The Invention of Difference

Acknowledgements

It is always surprising how many people are relied upon to get a book written and produced. The support of the partners – Kathryn Palmer, Nic Hammarling and Stuart Duff – has been invaluable. Realising that they gave this project their complete backing is immensely reassuring. We also had research support when we needed it from Susannah Gill and Ashley Williams. Then there is the team who got the book published – Mike Idziaszczyk and Laura Hollitzer. A great effort was put in by our book doctor, Paul May, who helped us shape, hone and polish the material. Finally thanks to Elizabeth Hill who helped us to understand the importance of the one commodity that we were short of: time.

Thank you one and all. It could not have happened without you.

Binna & Jo Kandola

The Invention of Difference

The story of gender bias at work

Pearn Kandola Publishing

Published by:

Pearn Kandola Publishing

9400 Garsington Road

Oxford

OX4 2HN

First published in Great Britain in 2013 by Pearn Kandola Publishing.

ISBN: 978-0-9562318-1-9

British Library Cataloguing in Publication Data
A catalogue record for this book is available from the British Library

Typeset in 9.5pt Formata

Printed in Great Britain by T J International, Padstow, Cornwall

Dedication

This book is dedicated to Renée and Grace.

"A thoroughly engaging read by an inspiring author. You will be hard pressed to find a better analysis of the impact of gender bias and therefore the fundamental importance of valuing difference."
Arun Batra, CEO National Equality Standard

"Binna Kandola is exceptional. Everything he writes is rooted in his long experience with real people in real situations which is what makes this book so relevant and timely."
Sir David Bell, Former Chairman of the Financial Times and a Non-Executive Director of The Economist

"This book is for all those people who think they are modern and have thrown off the shackles of bias and don't have any truck with stereotypes. Think again. This book on gender bias in the work place, couldn't be more timely. It challenges the so-called new assumptions about valuing the differences between men and women; differences which are just a re-arrangement of the old stereotypes. It is challenging and provocative, and every organisation interested in this subject should read it."

Razia Iqbal, BBC News Presenter

"Gender diversity is fundamental to our success yet real change is difficult to bring about. This book confirms the importance of requiring everyone to be open-minded and to challenge their fundamental beliefs about gender."
Ian Powell, Chairman and Senior Partner UK, PwC

"The Invention of Difference is a thought provoking contribution to the debate about gender equality. It challenges conventional views and argues for fundamental changes in the way we view the world. Required reading for those truly interested in gender equality."
The Right Honourable Baroness Prashar of Runnymede CBE, Deputy Chair of the British Council, former Chair of the Judicial Appointments Commission and former First Civil Service Commissioner

"Insightful and thought provoking analysis which brings a fresh and challenging perspective to the question of gender difference in the workplace."
Melanie Richards, KPMG Partner

"Few people are better equipped than Jo and Binna Kandola to demystify and debunk some of the things we think we know about so-called gender differences. If we are serious about raising the performance of our organisations, as well as making them fairer and better places to work, we will reflect on the lessons contained in this illuminating book, and act on them."
Stefan Stern, Visiting Professor in management practice at Cass Business School, London, and former FT columnist

Contents

Preface

ONE WORLD, ONE SPECIES

Until a few years ago, we knew of only the handful of planets in and around our solar system. We now know of thousands outside our solar system. Some researchers believe there is at least one planet circling every star in our galaxy. That's a minimum of 100 billion worlds, perhaps half of them rocky like ours.[1] Some of these may harbour life. But Earth may be the only one of those worlds in which the dominant species fancies that it is really two incompatible types of animal, with perspectives, insights and goals that are fundamentally unknowable across the divide. Even in the interludes that punctuate the war of the sexes, the two sides persist in their separation. We have made ourselves aliens. Humans – can't live with them, can't live without them.

Books that claim there are eternal and universal differences between the sexes are popular. We seem to recognise ourselves in them. But what we are really responding to is convenient stereotypes. "Typical man," we say, when a dexterous and technologically inclined man fails to work the washing machine. These books purport to tell us why women can't read maps or stick to the point of a story. The reward in reading books of this kind is a little like that of observational stand-up comedy – they are a kind of satire aimed at ourselves. We identify with the caricatures presented to us because this gives us a sense of belonging. We are licensed to excuse the faults and celebrate the talents guaranteed to us by our gender. A good dose of scientific-sounding narrative about natural selection, and preferably some brightly-coloured brain scans, and we're hooked.

The books that tell us women need to shed tears but men just need sheds play to our existing beliefs and reinforce well-established stereotypes. They make sense based on the ideologies we've been exposed to since birth, so we take them as truth. Although we characterise humans as learning animals, people are actually inclined to seek out information that will prove their existing hypotheses. We don't want to abandon what we already believe, so we are attracted to information that confirms our beliefs.

As the saying goes, people find what they look for, and the dangers of confirmation bias are well known in scientific disciplines. If a researcher already has a settled conviction about the phenomenon they are studying, then they won't pay attention to data that doesn't fit the conviction. Scientific trials have to be blind because researchers cannot be guaranteed to be blind. Experiments are designed specifically to eliminate bias and ensure repeatability by disinterested peers. We are not nearly so scrupulous in our day-to-day explorations of the world around us.

Given the absolute centrality of stereotypes to our habitual thought processes and our unconscious actions, the proposition of this book may be difficult for our minds to deal with. We will be presented with evidence that doesn't fit, so we'll want to ignore it. The key point to hold on to is this:

Personality and ability differences between men and women are not certain truths.

This approach is deeply antithetical to our preferred, habitual ways of interacting with the world. We all build theories all the time, guessing what other people want, what other people will do. But we are looking to be right, not wrong. It is easier and quicker this way because our minds love to take shortcuts.

Living on autopilot

In ordinary circumstances, we use the least mental effort necessary to achieve our current aims. We are, in the words of psychologists Susan Fiske and Shelly Taylor, "cognitive misers". It's as if our minds hoard our ideas, associations and stereotypes without wanting to let them go, or seek new ones.

Learning about facts that disconfirm our existing ideas can be difficult, uncomfortable and emotionally unrewarding. Every time a supposed fact is debunked, the world seems to become a little less familiar, a little more threatening. Adopting a contrary position on a subject of "common sense" can make a person stand out from a group and appear unsupportive. Social cohesion relies, after all, on unspoken agreement. So, pointing out that cracking your knuckles won't give you arthritis is one way of telling people that you are (a) pedantic, (b) humourless and (c) plain wrong. Likewise, doubting that testosterone is a kind of brain fuel for men, or opining that women make better soldiers, are acts of social failure. The passive reinforcement of existing beliefs exerted by our social surroundings chimes with the mind's preference for parsimonious and well-worn solutions.

Psychologists have repeatedly shown people's ability to dismiss evidence that does not match expectations. The most famous, and still one of the most entertaining, experiments in this field is the "invisible gorilla" experiment. Participants in the experiment are asked to watch a video of people moving around and passing basketballs to each other. The task is to count the passes. During the exercise, a person dressed in a gorilla suit walks among the players. The watchers don't see the gorilla, even though it is in plain sight, because their attention is focused on counting passes rather than recognising players.[2]

We seem to be able to screen out information which conflicts with our expectations or which is not relevant to the task in hand. The implications of the "invisible gorilla" effect are profound for any activity which requires monitoring for patterns. Unfortunately, unconscious bias is continually at work in our minds, leading us to ignore evidence that doesn't fit with what we are looking for. In this way, we do not notice the evidence of counter-stereotypical behaviour in those we deal with, but give over-generous weight to anything that bolsters a stereotype.

Humans, then, love to categorise and systematise. We are good at it, and it's at the heart of our evolutionary success. We organise our own thinking and we organise ourselves in groups.

Although these abstractions are intellectually sophisticated, the standards to which we operate with them are far from robust. We build elegant, finely graded systems for sorting people, but we don't notice what we're doing with those systems.

For a start, we make the logical error of assuming that a striking instance, or a set of similar instances, marks a categorical fact. We may believe that *all swans are white*, because we have only seen white swans – not knowing there are black swans in Australia. If we only grant swanhood to white swans, then, in our mental system, black swans are not swans at all. They are not only anomalous; they appear offensive to reason.

Research does show certain physical differences between men and women. But these differences are statistical rather than logical. So, on the whole, men are larger than women. However, there are clearly many women who are larger than many men. Statistical norms are useful for planning mass products or services. For example, you might build longer beds for the Scandinavian market than the Mediterranean market. This does not mean you should be surprised to meet a tall Italian or a short Swede. Although they are efficient from the production point of view, statistical norm-based solutions tend to reinforce stereotypes.

Here is a more formal illustration of the problem:

> Consider these two statements:
> A. "In our sample, we found a statistically significant difference in mean risk aversion between men and women, with women on average being more risk averse."
> B. "Women are more risk averse than men."

While the two statements are often taken as meaning the same thing, there is in fact a wide gulf of meaning between statement A, which is a narrow statement that can be factually correct within the confines of a particular study, and statement B, which is a broad statement that implies a stable characteristic of people according to their sex.[3]

From instance to generalisation, via statistics, stereotypes are nourished and reinforced by our speedy habits of thought.

Stereotyped thinking is self-reinforcing. A cognitive shortcut brings benefits in terms of faster decision-making, reduced periods of uncertainty and an overall sense of mastery over the situation. Each time we use a shortcut, we ingrain it a little deeper. And the deeper the ruts of our thinking grow, the harder it is to see beyond them.

Stereotyped thinking enables us to live on autopilot, negotiating our way through life as smoothly as possible. The more decisions we can take automatically, the more attention we can pay to what we deem to be really important. Even better, those automatic decisions don't even feel like decisions, because we expend no conscious effort on them. We reach for a canned judgement without knowing we are doing so, just as we slow down or change gear when we are driving. Our judgement machinery has all the appearance of instinct.

Challenging our beliefs and behaviours

Few of us would willingly agree that we are actively looking for support for our beliefs. Yet having our stereotypes challenged is uncomfortable. We may feel ashamed and defensive if we are called out on statements or actions that appear discriminatory. We don't consciously mean to be unfair. Unconscious bias has no moral sense. It takes place under the radar.

Nevertheless, we are attracted to messages that confirm and sanction the stereotypes in our private armouries. Anecdotes, articles and books which challenge gender stereotypes clash headlong with our deepest and most familiar beliefs. This makes them hard to engage with. Beliefs about gender are so central to our way of acting in the world that they don't even seem like beliefs. The conscious mind sees these beliefs as certain knowledge. To entertain an argument that runs counter to knowledge is a waste of time.

The first step in changing our behaviour therefore has to be recognising that our beliefs about gender are indeed beliefs and not true knowledge. We can then start to look at the evidence for our beliefs and question their validity.

Challenging the truth of existing beliefs is necessarily confrontational. For example, in order to assess the merits of Darwin's theory of evolution by natural selection, it's necessary to consider religion's account of creation as a matter of belief and not knowledge. Natural selection is still vehemently rejected in some communities, where the idea of nature as a blind and mechanical force offends beliefs in an original act of creation. And creationist beliefs "work" as well as Darwinian theory. Creationism does not explain nature as well as Darwinism from a scientific point of view. But, culturally, it will do. Creationism fits in a vast body of traditional practice and teaching that many people subscribe to as the basis of morality. Its social function is therefore very important – much more so than its scientific truth. So it is with gender.

Men and women have certain obvious physiological differences related to reproduction and the nurture of babies. But this is the full extent of the real differences between women and men. The physiological distinctions between women and men do not work systemically to influence features such as intelligence, skills or behaviour. It is not the case that women are flooded with "female" hormones that make them pliable and irrational; nor are men prey to "male" hormones that tug them towards cars and fights.

The basic physiological differences, transformed by culture, comprise what we call gender. Gender, then, is a social construction. The effects of gender in society are in turn a long way removed from nature's decision about organ allocation in mammals.

Why then do men and women appear to be so completely distinct? In this book we explore where modern-day beliefs about gender differences originate and how they operate in our day-to-day life at work. We also assess the evidence for non-physiological differences and how human nature is distorted – by we humans.

Why we wrote this book: gender equality at work

Gender at work remains a blind spot in most organisations. Gender equality is seen as a cause, and a peripheral one at that. We believe that issues of gender form the most fundamental and obstinate barriers to organisational effectiveness and individual happiness. Equality is more than a cause. It is a natural right that is being systematically denied to us – by ourselves.

We wrote this book to show that the concepts and culture of work that we all take for granted and treat as timeless and natural are really arbitrary, artificial conventions. By exploring the ways in which the orthodox gendered organisation has evolved, we can see how human motives have shaped our world of work. In seeing the hand of man (rarely woman) in the construction of work, we may be encouraged to make changes. The first step in changing work is owning the idea of work.

Can our businesses, government departments, schools and hospitals become places that serve and benefit men and women equally? Can we create organisations for people – regardless of their sex? We believe this is achievable. The power to make the change is in our heads. The world of work is what we think it is, what we say it is, and what we hear it is. If we can think, speak and hear anew, then we can make it new.

This book won't tell you how to get ahead if you're a woman. It won't beat you up if you're a man. It doesn't offer a tidy list of bullet points you can pin up on a wall.

But it will ask you to look afresh at work, to question what's taken for granted, and to ask "why not?" Our aim is to point out that many seemingly fixed and immutable features of work are unnecessary and dysfunctional. We use existing research to expose the facts about the gendered organisation and new psychological insights to suggest how organisations can change.

Gender equality is the natural state of women and men. Inequality is a cultural product created and maintained by people, consciously and unconsciously. It is learned behaviour. As such, it can be unlearned, or replaced by new learning.
Equality is a revolutionary idea, because it requires the removal or redesign of institutions and habits. But it is also a conservative idea. Equality seeks to return humanity to its full potential. This is a corrective movement.

Consider US Supreme Court judge Ruth Bader Ginsburg, who has worked consistently over many years for the cause of equal rights for women and men. The European Convention of Human Rights bans discrimination on the basis of sex in Britain. In the United States, a guarantee of equality was added to the Constitution in the Fourteenth Amendment, just after the Civil War. The amendment affirms that all US citizens are entitled to "the equal protection of the laws". However, when women cited the new amendment in order to claim the vote in Missouri, the Supreme Court ruled that this was a matter for the state. The Court continued to tolerate sex-based discrimination until Justice Ginsburg challenged the practice. She issued a dissenting opinion in 2007 when the Court disallowed a complaint by Lilly Ledbetter, who had discovered that she had been systematically underpaid for 15 years. One of President Obama's first actions in 2009 was to sign the Fair Pay Act into law.

Incidentally, Justice Ginsburg is also one of the people responsible for the contemporary use of the word "gender". Here's her account of one of those days in the office that created repercussions we're still processing today:

> In the seventies, I had a secretary, and she said, I've been typing this word sex, sex, sex, and let me tell you, the audience that you're addressing, the men that you are addressing – and they were all men in the appellate courts in those days – the first association of that word is not what you're talking about, so I suggest that you use a grammar book term: use the word gender. It will ward off distracting associations.[4]

The biological differences between men and women do not engender intellectual, social or moral differences. Men and women are the same. These facts ought to be self-evident. Their truth is obscured by the passive weight of tradition, but is also undermined by the active connivance of those who benefit most from the unequal status quo. The fight for equality is a very real fight that is being carried out in every area of human activity, often with little publicity. It's not just on the shop floor or in the call centre that people are striving for change – new ways of thinking are needed at every level, including the commanding heights of policy.

This book will explore where stereotypes and beliefs about the sexes originate and show that the gender inequality we find at work today has not always been present. We will cover the history of gender at work and how it has led to the idea that men and women are different. We will also consider the evidence for whether or not these differences are indeed real.

Our aim in this book is to debunk the view that the gendered world we see around us is the result of the "natural" differences between males and females; that biology has determined the outcome. We will show that – despite the obvious differences – we are remarkably similar and that therefore the differences we see between the genders at work are due to the world we have constructed. The message in this book may feel a little bleak to some, but it is one filled with optimism: because the gendered workplace has been constructed by us, it is perfectly within our power to deconstruct and recreate it. That is, of course, if we want to.

As the comedian George Carlin said: "Men are from Earth and women are from Earth. Get over it."

A note on the text

We use "they" and "them" instead of "he" and "she". This may offend grammar purists. If so, that's all to the good. If we can change the way we talk about gender, we can change the way we behave too.

References

1. Available at: http://news.nationalgeographic.co.uk/news/billions-of-earthlike-planets-found-in-milky-way/. Accessed 19 September 2013.

2. The Invisible Gorilla: And Other Ways Our Intuitions Deceive Us. *theinvisiblegorillacom*. Available at: http://www.theinvisiblegorilla.com/videos.html. Accessed 19 September 2013.

3. Nelson JA. Are Women Really More Risk-Averse than Men? Global Development and Environment Institute Working Paper No. 12-05, September 2012. Available at: http://ase.tufts.edu/gdae/Pubs/wp/12-05NelsonRiskAverse.pdf. Accessed 19 September 2013.

4. BBC Radio 4, Law In Action, 12 March 2013.

1

HOW WE BUILT BUSINESS AS USUAL

Ideas about the roles of women and men at work are intertwined with the meaning of work itself. Where did "work" come from, and how has it developed – or not – over the generations? Is work natural or artificial? Work has a complex and colourful history of its own. This chapter and the next look at where work came from – and why we're stuck with it.

What we consider today to be work is relatively new. Also, the notion of a job as a separate part of life, or as an identity that individuals inhabit on certain days of the week, certain hours of the day and in certain settings, is a comparatively recent phenomenon. The concept of the job is firmly anchored in a complex cluster of significant concepts, such as the political ideal of full employment, the social validation that jobs bring ("What do you do?"), and the organisation of life streams around jobs – training before, pensions and care after.

"Jobs" rush into the space created by the work–life split. They mediate between people and tasks. A new domain of power, control, conflict and opportunity grows in this newly defined space. And eventually we're all just "living for the weekend".

Work has never been a simple, single facet of human life nor a neutral topic of study: "work itself has a history, changing in nature and understanding, just as language, customs and fashions have changed throughout the ages."[1]

Our relationship with work, then, has at best been ambiguous – with work seen as something that has to be endured, if not enjoyed. In ancient Greece, for example, work was carried out exclusively by slaves. Slaves were not part of the city state or *polis*: they did not count as citizens. Politics – the affairs of the *polis* – were valued above all else and anyone who worked was by implication ignoble. The Greeks had no single word for work, but three related words: *ponos,* meaning a painful activity; *ergon*, meaning a military or agricultural task; and *techne*, from which we get our word "technique." None of these words refers to roles, relationships or rewards, three of the ideas central to our contemporary conceptual cluster of work.

Revealingly, some modern words for work derive from the "painful" portion of the ancient vocabulary. The French word *travail* derives from the Latin *tripalium*, a torture device made of three stakes to which a victim was tied before being burned.[1,2] The English word "travail" has the same origins. The American spelling of *labor* is identical to its Latin source, which means toil or trouble. Our word "work" can be traced back to the Greek *ergon* and beyond to *varazem*, a word from ancient Iran.

Our contemporary notion of work as "productive activities" that fill time would have been unrecognisable to people in earlier times, when (what we would call) work stopped as soon as its aim had been achieved. Yet abundance and scarcity of resources do not seem to be the determining factors in the organisational structures of early societies. While the environment dictates what is possible, people design what is permissible.

For us today, "work" can also have connotations of creativity. We talk about the works of great composers, while expressive activities including acting and psychotherapy are often given this creative sense of work. In classical society, craft workers who produced items for other people, or items based on the ideas or requirements of other people, were not seen as creative workers. As Greek society became more consumerist, the craft worker came to be seen more and more as merely the performer of a labour process, rather than the originator of a product.

Work versus employment

Although they are often used interchangeably – especially by economists and politicians – work and employment are contradictory concepts. Work provides meaning, status and a way of fulfilling oneself. Work can be noble, uplifting and energising. Employment, on the other hand, is a matter of necessity. It can be dehumanising and can abstract us from life.

Our word *employ* means "use". It ultimately derives, via Latin *implicare*, to proto-Indo-European words to do with folding something inside something else. There is a buried sense, then, that to employ something is to capture it or enclose it – to engulf its independence. In modern language, we can often substitute "use" for "employ" with no loss of meaning. The implication (a word from the same Latin root) is that employees are used. They are useful; they are tools. Today we are less likely to talk about factory or field "hands" but "heads" in "roles": people fill the spaces defined by nodes on a process chart.

But not all work–life activity is dignified with the name of work. Keith Grint defines work in this way:

> Work tends to be an activity that transforms nature and is usually undertaken in social situations, but exactly what counts as work depends upon the interpretation of powerful groups.[2]

Those with power – the master, the guild or the management guru – decides what counts as work. Since men have the power, "women's work" has traditionally been regarded as non-work. Domestic labour has long been treated as less important than paid work, and the slogan "wages for housework" is designed to change attitudes to domestic labour – although if this ever did happen it would, ironically, only serve to reinforce the view that a woman's place is in the home.

Work also has a strong moral dimension. Yet the moral value of doing a job well for its own sake is a relatively recent development. For most of human history, work has been both hard and degrading. Working hard in the absence of compulsion was not the norm in Hebrew, classical or medieval cultures.[3] The Judeo-Christian belief system, which had such a huge influence on Western culture and civilisation, took a different attitude to work. Man had been placed by God in the Garden of Eden, according to Genesis "to work and take care of it" – creation being nothing more than a kind of one-person full employment programme. The scheme was ruined when sin entered the garden because of the woman's weakness, and humans were evicted. Mankind's punishment was the curse of working to survive. This is the deep background to the standard Western belief that work is necessary to prevent poverty and destitution.

The way to salvation was religion and spirituality but the intertwining of work and belief found further expression with the rise of Protestantism and the translation of the Bible into modern European languages. Access to the text of the Bible via Gutenberg's newly invented printing press changed people's attitudes to religion and religion's relationship to everyday life. While the teaching of the Bible continued to be respected, the guidance of priests began to be substituted by a commonly shared code of ethics based on frugality and hard work.

Attitudes changed in the times of Martin Luther and John Calvin, when the status of work was revised from necessity to moral duty.[1] In a letter to his son, Hans, Luther instructed him "to work hard, pray well and be good"[4] – the link between religion, morality and work is clear. This line of thought informed the Victorians: Samuel Smiles, for example, taught that "Heaven helps those who help themselves". The famous Protestant work ethic shaped work structures and practices for many generations to come, to the point where it "is beginning to take on the character of a stranglehold no longer simply colouring our views but choking judgement".[1] The knot made by the combination of Biblical authority, traditional practice and a common ideology proves to be strong and durable.

For most of human history, most people worked or they starved. Since the Industrial Revolution, for the majority of people work must also be done via employment, otherwise it is worthless. To be without employment is to have a questionable existence:

> Unemployment is not a category that would be recognised outside a very limited slice of space and time; that it is today, and that the label is crucial to the status of the individual, tells us as much about the kind of society we inhabit as about the kind of individual stigmatised.[2]

Work, then, tells us who we are and how we fit in. It defines our broad moral value – whether we are "strivers" or "skivers". Work is both our punishment for being alive, and our means of making a living. From its distillation in the mythical mists of time and rise to prominence during the agrarian period, work has come to define people – and to separate people into women and men.

The mists of time or Theory YDD

When it comes to looking far back in time, we know much more about the distribution of different types of pollen or the concentration of CO_2 in the atmosphere than we do about the thought patterns of our earliest ancestors. Skeletons can tell us about diet, but not about the role of food in everyday life. Grave goods can tell us that status differentials existed, but not the hierarchies involved. Earthworks will reveal where a family lived, but not how they loved.

We humans are categorising animals. We use categories to simplify the choices we have to make, to enable complex thinking and to organise our surroundings. When presented with a new piece of information, we like to pigeonhole it as rapidly as possible. We will make up a category if one isn't immediately available.

Categorisation is closely allied to our interest in stories. Deciding whether something belongs in one category or another, or defining a new category, requires a kind of narrative. Something belongs in a particular category because of some notable feature, some habitual usage, or some authoritative advice. People believe that every collection of events can be made sense of by appealing to a narrative thread. This is, of course, a good thing because it leads to scientific enquiry. But it also leads to what is kindly called folk wisdom – with its embedded superstition, error and prejudice.

Gender is particularly susceptible to the narrative charms of "just so" stories. These stories often masquerade as science, when they are really speculation. The mists of time can be very useful for concocting origins, especially racial ones. The same mists blur the formation of ideas about gender. Just as any ancient tribe of interest seems to have arrived from somewhere else, so "gender" appears to have been always with us. Prehistory – the many thousands of years during which human beings recorded their activities sporadically and by accident – is an area peculiarly open to fabrication, both intentional and unintentional. Where there is no text to read, it's easier to read a story into the evidence.

Evolutionary stories are interpretations, selective and seemingly as compelling as any brightly-coloured image of a brain scan. They have more or less plausibility depending on the preconceptions of the audience. This means that successful stories – ones that gain traction and repetition – can be designed by selecting features that fit the audience's expectations.

These apparently scientific arguments from evolutionary processes also tend to be deterministic – we are the way we are because we have always been like this. That is to say, not only are evolutionary explanations for current behaviours or values taken to be inevitable, they are also chosen to promote certain interpretations above the alternatives.

We create a past to explain the present. A BBC radio programme, *Fighting the Power of Pink,* explored why females prefer the colour pink and males blue. One explanation provided by a psychologist relies on evolution: men as hunters had to be able to see objects against the sky and women as gatherers had to pick berries. What's wrong with this story? Quite a lot. First, we're asked to agree that women prefer pink. Whether or not women were discovered to favour pink, this wouldn't tell us whether their preference was natural. Perhaps a preference for pink, where it exists, has been inculcated by the tireless machinations of the Disney princesses. Other contributors explained that the differences between the genders on colour preferences were very small – so by no means do all men prefer blue and women pink. Certainly, pink was regarded as a masculine colour prior to the twentieth century.

Second, we're asked to agree that women would have been gatherers and that the roles are fixed and enduring. And, seriously, when we give this a moment's thought, how hard is it to spot something against the sky? And have you ever seen a pink berry – blueberries yes, blackberries even, nice, ripe *red* strawberries – but pink? This is a back-projection of later gender divisions on to earlier ways of life. Third, the explanation provided excludes other possible explanations and in so doing creates a sense of certainty about something that is eminently contestable.

Evolutionary theory is a marvellous rhetorical tool for explaining away inequalities. Here, for example, is Nigel Nicholson commenting on the scarcity of women in leadership positions: "Domination, competition and patriarchy are biologically encoded as our model of authority."[5] Can a mental model really be "biologically encoded"? If so, where is this code? Certainly, our inherited model of authority evolved. But it's a product of culture which has to be taught and learned.

The most popular view of the early history of humankind goes like this: males go out and hunt for days or weeks at a time while the females stay home, looking after the children and collecting herbs – waiting for the men to bring home the bacon. This leads us to think it's right that women should be nurses, teachers and carers, while men will be engineers, doctors, lawyers and leaders. We call this Theory YDD – for Yabba Dabba Doo.

For adherents of this view, and there are many, *The Flintstones* isn't a cartoon but a reality documentary. Fred, Wilma, Barney and Betty are us and we are them. Theory YDD, in other words, is a projection of contemporary dominant values on to a distant and ultimately unknowable prehistory. The same agenda is urged less directly when people claim women are (or believe they are) better multi-taskers than men, or say that men have (or believe they have) a better sense of direction. Since these generalisations are themselves false, the evolutionary tale-telling that supposedly explains them is redundant.

It's not true that prehistoric and modern people are interchangeable. Up until the Industrial Revolution, the family worked as a unit. Tribes in prehistory were often nomadic. Women hunted and men cultivated. In fact, it may be more accurate to describe these groups as gatherer-hunters. We can't picture this way of life, so we say the way we are now is the way we've always been.

Anthropological studies of peoples following traditional ways of life give us an idea of how life might really have been. A portrait of the native American Ojibwa from the 1930s shows that although there were divisions of work by gender, there were also many examples of "women going beyond their prescribed roles". Gender roles therefore existed but were not rigid: "Everywhere there are some women who hunt, go to war and doctor as men do."[6]

Theory YDD then is a very lazy approach to the human condition and tends to telescope vast periods of time into simple continuities. The way we think today seems to us to be the way people have always thought, even though we have no proof that it is.

Work in agrarian societies

When hunter-gatherer societies began to farm, leaving their nomadic habits for part or all of the year, their attitudes towards life and work necessarily changed. Every society creates work in its own image, adding new layers of practice and meaning to its social inheritance. It is at this stage that human society starts becoming patriarchal in some parts of the world.

Men are on average physically stronger and so can assert dominance. Women lactate and are abstracted from the working environment while they are feeding. As a consequence of their superior strength, men are deemed to be of a higher status than women. These physical facts became generalised as the idea that men and women are different. Status, then, ultimately creates gender. Patrolling and reinforcing the gender divide, as we discuss further in Chapter 4 when we consider prescribed stereotypes, maintains inequalities of status – to the obvious benefit of men.

Man may not always have been in charge, despite his greater bulk. Women, after all, were the only real creators: the givers of life. Lithuanian-American archaeologist Marija Gimbutas found evidence for matriarchal pre-Indo-

European societies. These gynocentric or matristic societies, which focused on the worship of female deities, were replaced by invading patriarchal societies in the Bronze Age.[7] Much early art depicts goddesses, suggesting at the very least a communal respect for female fertility. It is possible also to detect the afterlife of the matriarchal goddesses not only in the classical pantheon, but in the cult of the Virgin Mary (who, by the way, wears blue, not pink). Beyond the Indo-European area, evidence has also been found for matriarchal societies in Africa and China.[7] Desmond Morris, the zoologist and author, has said that he feels "disturbed and angry" at the way women are treated in our age. He says: "To me, as a zoologist who has studied human evolution, this trend towards male domination is simply not in keeping with the way in which *homo sapiens* have developed over millions of years."[8]

In Morris's view, this shift from equality to the domination of men was in large part due to religion:

> In ancient times the great deity was always a woman, but then, as urbanisation spread, She underwent a disastrous sex change, and in simple terms the benign Mother Goddess became the authoritarian God and Father. With a vengeful male God to back them up, ruthless holy men through the ages have ensured their own affluent security and the higher social status of men in general, at the expense of women who sank to a low social status that was far from their evolutionary birthright.

A possible pre-patriarchical tradition is visible in the carved figures known as Sheela na gigs, which are found in churches, castles and towers in Ireland and Britain. The figure is a naked woman, opening her vulva. They are usually placed over doors or windows. Comedian Stewart Lee visited one such site in Shropshire:

> The priest took me outside to point out a haunting and all but eroded figure above a now bricked-up entrance, her legs wide open to the north wind. "In the old days people liked their coffins to enter the church through this doorway," he said, "and that way the dead got the blessing of the new God, and perhaps the blessing of the old goddess too."[9]

The first evidence we have in Britain for an organised society with work-related social roles comes from the Roman period. Roman Britain conjures up an image of unnaturally straight roads and fancy foreign bath houses. The reality for most people in Britain for this period – which lasted more than 400 years – was subsistence farming. Britain's domestic product consisted of agricultural commodities, hunting dogs, timber, precious metals, pig iron and slaves.[2] The shift to a feudal society after the fall of the Roman Empire led to the addition of security payments to the basic agricultural model. The pain of work was here to stay.

A life of toil

Before the Industrial Revolution, there was little in the way of formal division of labour, by gender or any other criterion. Work was not conducted or imposed by any coercive authority. With all production carried out by hand, most tasks were carried out independently and performed in the family setting. People worked to their own rhythms and sold their goods at market. "Work–life balance" wasn't an issue because work and life were not distinguished from each other. The "nine to five" didn't exist because no one was tied to the clock.

Going further back, hunter-gatherer (or gatherer-hunter) societies made no distinction between work and non-work. The division between these types of activity is socially constructed, rather than natural. Hunting and gathering were certainly fundamental to existence, but neither was regarded as work:

> Would the Neanderthal have the same way of thinking as those of us who were reared in households where the nearest thing to hunter-gatherers are those whom we describe as the breadwinners?[1]

Women carried out a far greater range of roles before the Industrial Revolution than after it, up to the present day. In agrarian societies, men and women both carried out what is now considered men's work and women's work. Women could look after pigs and chickens, the dairy, manage kitchen gardens and orchards, and keep the proceeds from their sales. Men were responsible for grain and cattle because these were more valuable commodities. The

Fig 1.1: Women building city walls from Christine de Pizan, Le Livre de la Cite des Dames (early 15th century).

demarcation doesn't arise from different abilities, but from status. Over time, such informal divisions become solidified as traditional roles.[10]

It is true that women have typically carried out the lower-paid, lower-status work, but there was more interchangeability before the industrial age. Men would carry out what could be broadly described as "horsework", including going to market, which might involve travelling long distances.[10] This work was seen as of higher status but when the men were away, women would naturally take over these activities. In the thirteenth century it would not have been unusual to see women employed as carpenters, masons and coopers. By the sixteenth century they were practically non-existent in these occupations.[2] An evolutionary, deterministic argument could be found for this change, we are sure, but a social and cultural one, the rise of the guilds throughout Europe, is the most compelling.

Nor have women always been at the bottom of the pile as employees in the workforce hierarchy. Men have always been top and women second, but there was a time when children were last. Families worked together and children were expected to make their contribution. The notion of a "breadwinner", therefore, and a male one at that, is a relatively new one and did not exist prior to the Industrial Revolution. The "family wage" was all-important and in this simple expression we can see the interrelated and interdependent relationships between members of a household.

For example, the way we view children today is a recent phenomenon. Placing the child at the centre of concern began as a late Romantic fashion:

> The childhood of a French nobleman in the eighteenth century
> was not usually the period of his life upon which he looked
> back with either affection or regret. The doctrine that parents
> exist for the sake of their children was not then accepted, and
> the loving care and hourly attention bestowed upon the
> children of today would have appeared ridiculous to sensible
> people. When Rousseau, the first man of sentiment,
> abandoned all his children, one after the other, to be brought
> up as unknown foundlings, his conduct was thought odd but
> not vile.[11]

At the other end of the social scale, children were regarded as small adults. They therefore worked. "Childhood" is a luxury we have earned with the growth of leisure.

The strong moral imperative that people now identify with caring for children is neither universal nor eternal. But it is real, because we have made it so. We are more than happy to agree that attitudes to children have changed but, when it comes to gender, we prefer to believe that these patterns of behaviour are fixed, natural and somehow true.

Women may always have run the household but this was a very different role from that of the housewife as we conceive it today. A woman's contribution to the family wage was valued. A saying from Bremen in Germany expresses this: "Where a woman doesn't work there is no bread on the table." The same sentiments were articulated in France: "No wife, no cow, hence no milk, no cheese, nor hens, nor chickens, nor eggs".[10]

Specialisms and the status that went with them have existed for some time. The guild system organised trades and crafts around entry conditions and quality standards. The origins of guilds can be traced back to the first century AD and the Collegium Fabrorum – the guild of smiths – in Chichester.[2] Such organisations live on in our contemporary professional associations. Someone seeking to ply a controlled trade would have to go through the stages of apprentice, journeyman and master.

Guilds developed in many forms throughout Europe, with the common aim of jealously guarding access to skills. These organisations did not just control entry into professions, but regulated wages and set standards for quality. In this way, the establishment of guilds provided part of the foundations needed for regular trade. Within the guild, masters passed on the "mystery" to learners – the original Greek source of this word, *mustērion*, refers to the domain of secrecy into which initiates of a cult entered. Being apprenticed obviously involved being taught the skills, but it also involved creating a sense of inclusion and belonging to something that others were to be excluded from.[10]

However, the guild system proved unworkable in the Industrial Revolution. Production centred in factories or mines demanded a different approach to the recruitment, development and control of labour. Recognition of this fact leads ultimately to modern management.

Splitting work, splitting people

The formal separation of work and leisure began with the Industrial Revolution, a massive and rapid social change which effectively split people's identities between home and workplace. This social upheaval is an important context for the development of gender.

The Industrial Revolution heralded not only changes in production methods but changes in attitudes to work too. Populations had grown, cities had expanded and the number of poor people had increased. Those outside the guild system were to become the new labour force on which the economy would come to depend. The work was deskilled and routine but it also required a different sense of discipline from employees: you can leave your animals for a time, but a furnace needs attention.

Although it is true that women had lower status than men, they were nevertheless involved in a wider range of roles and occupations before the Industrial Revolution than at any time since. As we have seen, before the Industrial Revolution high-status trades were controlled by guilds, which effectively excluded women from the better jobs. But women still had roles to play. So, for example, women were not allowed to do leather work, but they could make buckles. Since buckles are generally made from metal, this meant that women could be metal-workers.

During the Industrial Revolution women were to be found working in four principal areas:

- Traditional occupations such as spinning

- Assisting men in their work

- The less profitable industries where they were used as cheaper workers to keep costs down

- The industries and roles that were less skilled and which needed little training.[10]

In other words, the roles assigned to women were not as prescriptive or narrow before the Industrial Revolution as they were after it.

The European pattern was also discernible in the United States. The early settlers had strong religious beliefs and it was because of these that women were expected to work. The Protestant work ethic was such a part of their identity it became known the Yankee Ethic.[4] As in Europe, the settler females undertook a wide range of roles pre-industrialisation. When looking for spouses both men and women valued physical strength highly. Even during the early years of industrialisation, American women were involved in publishing newspapers, running distilleries and managing inns.[6] In England at the start of the nineteenth century, more middle-class women were involved in commerce than in any other profession.[10]

The Industrial Revolution also led to the systematic removal of women from the workplace. This was achieved by a combination of changed societal attitudes towards the appropriate roles for men and women, new legislation and the role of the unions. This period saw a noticeable shift in attitudes to women, with their role becoming increasingly idealised and focused on the home and family. By mid-century the world had changed to one that is more recognisable to us today.

During the Industrial Revolution "labour" was identified as a category for the first time. Labour then became organised in the form of unions, themselves an evolution of the guilds. By the late 1880s, however, only 1% of women were in unions.[2] Their position therefore was very weak, with some unions going on strike to keep women out of their areas of work.

Industrial processes need to be coordinated, so it was important that people turned up for their shifts on time and paced their work to the rhythm of the master process. This led to a new attitude towards time. Hours of the day became more important, whereas features of the season receded. People's behaviour was regulated on a much smaller scale, with the day being structured for them and managed on an hour-by-hour or even minute-by-minute basis. This led to new moral attitudes – or, more accurately, the reinforcement and application of a particular moral code newly enshrined as an ideal. Drinking, for example, was not perceived as much of a problem in purely agricultural societies, since being somewhat drunk didn't necessarily impede the tasks of farming. Drunkenness in a factory setting, on the other hand, is potentially lethal.[12]

The moral focus extended to parental roles in bringing up children. The apparently neutral term *parent* comes, for practical purposes, to mean mother, since women are given the responsibility for childcare. Laws were enacted in many countries to restrict the hours women and children could work – and to protect male employment. While such changes were taking place supposedly in support of the family, men's work remained largely brutalised.

By looking at what happened during the development of work, we can see how a new system, and its associated model of thinking, emerged. For example, the systematisation of work created a new distinction between work and leisure. This distinction between work and non-work is important. No longer was work inextricably linked to the direct needs of the family; people worked to earn a wage and were productive. To be unwaged therefore suggested a lower status. Increasingly, the great and the good saw a woman's role to be in the home.

Men in all parts of society became united in the view that women should be at home. Lord Ashley, speaking in the House of Lords, believed that women working was "disturbing the order and the rights of the labouring men by ejecting the males from the workshop and filling their places with females, who are thus withdrawn from all their domestic duties and exposed to the insufferable toil at half the wages that would be assigned to males, for the support of their families." At the same time the Trades Union Congress (TUC) had the very same concerns. "It was their duty," said Henry Broadhurst of the TUC in 1877, "as men and husbands to bring about a condition of things, where wives could be in their proper sphere at home, instead of being dragged into competition for livelihood against the great and strong men of the world."[10]

So the concern for women working long hours in factories was also inextricably linked with the concern about men being out of work. In addition, the appalling working conditions and lower wages meant that being at home was a more attractive alternative for working-class women. But there was little concern for the work that women had to do in the home to earn a wage. Factories regularly put work out to women working from their homes – a system operated in Europe, Canada and the United States.

With women, most notably married women, now at home, the idea of the family wage diminished, to be replaced by the ideal of the male breadwinner. This created a new rhythm to the day, and when combined with ideals about gender roles, led to strictures about men's and women's work. The woman's day is different from that of the man. Typically, the man goes out to work and the woman stays at home – so the world is effectively divided into separate male and female domains. The woman is expected to clean the house, care for the children and feed the breadwinner. The notion of a family income and economy is replaced by the idea that only the man's work is significant or even real.

With the stabilisation of the Industrial Revolution in northern and western Europe, North America and beyond, the attitudes to work established during industrialisation became the new tradition within and against which individuals thought and acted. As fields of employment extended beyond manual labour into service industries and administrative activities, the exclusion of women was carried over from the early industrial model. In Britain and Germany, but not France, marriage bars were introduced: if you were female and you married then you were out of a job. In Britain married women were barred from the civil service between 1876 and 1946. However, many women supported this kind of ban. Middle-class women typically wanted to "retire" to a married life – and not be "left on the shelf" like an unwanted product. Career-minded women supported this situation because it made for reduced competition for promotion.[2] Working-class women were also encouraged to pursue marriage above work. The financial benefits associated with marriage were necessary for setting up a home.

At the same time there was increased pressure for women to focus on their roles as mothers. The editorial writer of *The Times* in 1907 worked himself up to fever pitch, linking the demands for women's emancipation with their biological role: "The rights of women increase. But what is their greatest duty – to give birth, to give birth again, always to give birth... Should a woman refuse to give birth, she no longer deserves her rights."[10] (Our so-called, and totally misnamed, "family-friendly" policies are, it could be argued, merely reinforcing the fact that flexible working is only permissible if a woman has fulfilled her "greatest duty".) If the expectations of women weren't clear enough, in France and Germany women were given medals for the number of children they produced and in Italy the government granted additional allowances depending on the number of children they bore.[7]

In the United States, debates were taking place in the press as to what roles were appropriate for women to undertake. One editorial, referring to a specific occupation that women wished to enter, began by saying that "[W]e should honor them for their sympathy and humanity." However, females should not be allowed to carry out this job because any man who has worked with women "cannot shut his eyes to the fact that they, with the best intentions in the world, are frequently a useless annoyance." Any guesses as to the profession he was talking about? Nursing.[6] What is now seen as the quintessential woman's profession was once anything but.

Housework also came in for redefinition and took on the meaning and shape we use today. In France, *le ménage* did not refer to housework but to the management of the whole farm. In Germany, the *Hausmutter* shared her tasks with the *Hausvater*. There was status and standing associated with both roles. But over the years the scope of the *Hausmutter's* role was steadily restricted until it became the *Hausfrau* of today. In Britain and North America, housewifery, a term used since the thirteenth century, was equated to househusbandry, and involved the responsibility for management of the household in its widest sense.[10] The term "housework" doesn't appear in the English language until the mid-1800s.

Prior to the Industrial Revolution, property delineated distinctions of class. With industrialisation, cleanliness assumed a much higher priority. "Cleanliness is next to godliness" as the old saying goes, and so the type of activity women should be focusing on in the home became more clearly defined.

Gender roles therefore became much more sharply defined in the workplace and in the home. To many, this was as things should be and represented a return to the natural order of life. This was emphasised by popular publications of the time. In Britain, there was Isabella Mary Beeton's *Household Management*; in Germany Henriette Davidis's *Die Hausfrau*; in France an equivalent work by Simon Bloquel called *Guide des femmes de ménage, des cuisinieres et des bonnes enfants.* These all appeared from 1859 to 1863 and today around the world bookshelves and news-stands are full of advice to women on how to carry out and fulfil their natural, predetermined role.[10] A century and a half of human progress seems to have left the ideal of womanhood stranded in a perpetual struggle against dirt and the unsatisfied hunger of her charges.

Working the system: the rise of the professions

Traditional forms of work and ways of working were replaced by new methods and new occupations which organised themselves into the professional bodies we see around us today. In Europe, the United States, Canada, Australia and Japan between 1850 to 1920, engineers, accountants, architects, lawyers and so on developed the professional institutions that are still with us today. These bodies served as a means of advancing technical skills and knowledge but also acted as barriers to entry for any newcomers. Formal education requirements were needed to enter these professions, creating another barrier to women, as they were denied access to higher education. These changes took place while women were being removed from the workplace, so it is no surprise that these occupations were, and to a great extent still are, male-dominated.

The development of work since the Industrial Revolution can be seen as a steady process of formalisation and systematisation. The evolving rules about work, about who should be doing what and how, developed in an apparently more objective and "scientific" manner than before industrialisation. The scientific management movement equated employees with tools. The approach, often known as Taylorism after the pioneer Frederick Taylor (1856–1915), aimed to match people, tasks and tools in the most effective manner, so that no time, effort, power or materials were wasted. The time and motion man, with his clipboard and stopwatch, goes together with the image of Charlie Chaplin becoming a cog in the machine of Modern Times. Today, descendants of the scientific management approach include business process (re)engineering and various flavours of "lean" management.

By the late nineteenth century an entirely new class of profession was being created, and one that is easily overlooked: management. In the fifty-year period from 1880 to 1930 the United States was instrumental in inventing management. In 1880 the shelves of the New York Public Library held no books on management. By 1910, it held 240. The first management school opened in Philadelphia in 1881. But the sociologist Yehouda Shenhav is more specific still: management is the creation of American engineers.[13]

The philosophy behind management as a discipline is dominated by engineering thinking and the rise of management coincides with the rise of the engineer. In 1800 there were fewer than 30 engineers in the United States. In 1880 there were 3,000 and by 1930 there were 300,000. The majority of these, approximately two-thirds, eventually ended up in management.[13] Not only was engineering – and, consequently, management – male, it was also elitist since the upper middle classes dominated. American management systems appeared rational, scientific and ordered. The rise of this methodology took place during a time of industrial unrest and uncertainty. The creation of systems to regulate all functions, not just production, was seen as a way of ensuring fairness as well as predictability.

Systems thinking is rooted in control – of the production of goods and services, and the people involved. By rethinking people as parts of a system, or a machine, it is easier to deskill them. From an engineering point of view, reducing the need for human intervention leads to greater efficiency and therefore higher profits.

As the systems approach developed and was imitated across industry, so bureaucracy grew in its wake. Organising assets, processes and people requires record keeping and checking. Supervision and reporting are needed to verify that the system is working properly and to provide evidence for ways in which its performance might be improved. With bureaucracy comes a whole new kind of power: the power to obstruct and delay, to build empires, and to buy and sell favours. This is why bureaucracies tend to grow their own meta-bureaucracies. The checkers need to be checked too.

From the perspective of individual experiences and the social environment, bureaucracy has the effect of not just standardising work but of homogenising it. Jobs in a mill are all physically the same, because the machines demand stylised movements and drive the pace of work. But the jobs also become standardised in their non-mechanical aspects. Employees must conform to the demands of the system: when they show up, when they leave, how they engage with the tasks that fill the interim. The control systems were increasingly elaborate and in some cases included mystifying rules and regulations that sought to ensure that no deviancy from them was tolerated. If the rule said that no books were allowed in the factory that meant no books – not even the Bible. So while work was being linked to morality it could conveniently be decoupled from religion if it got in the way. Reliability, order and control were the order of the day.

This approach did not and indeed could not allow individuality. "Just suppose each man in your book-keeping department had his own way; suppose each clerk in your ordering department had his own individual kind of order blank, and each man in the stock room had his own system of scoring, handling and accounting. And suppose these men told you they had as much right to be individual."[13] In effect, the system knows best. Individual expression and variance are not to be permitted as these would amount to an attack on efficiency and the system itself.

The systems built in the industrial age are not just the foundation of our modern economy. They are deeply embedded in the fabric of our lives. We may tell ourselves we live in a post-industrial, postmodern, information age, but we still operate with the engineering mindset that built our world. The systems we invented to scale up economic activities now hinder our ability to change. Goals such as greater agility, or the need to be more customer-centric, or the desire to run more sustainable processes, are obstructed by the system-derived categories that structure all our thinking.

Systematisation turned abstract ideals into prescriptive norms. That is, what was once thought of as "right" but perhaps unattainable began to be seen as not only attainable but basic to life. So, although there were always ideals about what men and women were supposed to do, the success of systematisation translated these notions into something like social laws. The process of management defines what a job is, how it is to be carried out and when. When this is coupled with societal prescriptions about the roles of men and women, we see that the world we have now emerged at that time.

We trained ourselves to accept these systems and now we are, largely unwittingly, in thrall to them. How can we retrain our brains to make new worlds possible? We need to break the connections that have solidified around gender and behaviour, status and roles.

In a system, an element has one function, and only one function. It has defined relationships with other components. It does not suddenly start performing another task, or helping another component, or taking the afternoon off. Our world today is much more fluid and unpredictable. It is also much more focused on the needs of individuals rather than the production of products and services for the masses.

The system that's embedded in our brains doesn't match current reality. It therefore inhibits our functioning. You could say that we are running the wrong software — software created by males with a leaning towards engineering principles. Engineers won the race to define the nature of work. Their successes produced the infrastructure on which we still rely: railways, metalled roads, the electricity grid, potable water, sewerage — and money. Their attitudes infected every other branch of activity.

The First and Second World Wars

The two world wars of the twentieth century introduced total war to the nations involved. Unlike earlier conflicts, which might leave most members of the

Fig 1.2: A woman working on an aircraft propeller World War 1.

community unaffected, these wars demanded the full resources of each country. Throughout Europe, men were enlisted to fight, creating shortages of manpower that had to be filled by women.

This arrangement was seen as extraordinary and temporary. With much of the skilled male population drafted into the services, new sources of labour were needed to produce armaments and fuels for the war effort, and to maintain vital infrastructure including the railways. The trade unions wanted to ensure that any lowering of entry standards was purely temporary. Unskilled workers were given rapid training courses that enabled them to do the skilled work normally controlled by the unions. This was known as "dilution". The "dilutees" were overwhelmingly female.

The perspective of "dilution" is of course wholly male. The wartime labour situation is more complex when viewed from a more neutral angle. For example, the outbreak of the First World War actually led to a dramatic rise in female unemployment as short time working was introduced. In some sectors such as textiles, employment fell 43% in the first few months of the war[14]. Women, then, were already significantly represented in the world of work and the initial effect of the war was to drive down wages. Dilution and "substitution" – where the skills of the original and replacement worker were equal – referred to the oddity of women performing in male roles, such as heavy labour.

The sudden visibility of women doing "men's work" during the First World War offered a striking alternative model for women who hardly lacked information or advice about their traditional roles. The propaganda of the time emphasised the different and discontinuous nature of this period as there had been nothing like it in the industrial era.[14]

Despite assurances that the use of women in male workplaces was strictly temporary, the strikes that occurred during the First World War were often sparked by resentment of dilutees and their encroachment on incumbents' territory. Employers tended to sympathise with the male workers.[2]

During the Second World War, new provisions were made to ensure women could work in factories. The measures included workplace nurseries and crèches. These were provided to a level not seen before – or since. The British were particularly successful in mobilising women. In 1943, workplace facilities could accommodate a quarter of the children of female war workers.[2]

However, female absenteeism was high. The duties of childcare combined with the need to queue for food and manage rations competed for women's time. The government encouraged "neighbourhood shopping leagues" and women were often given unofficial time off to shop. When these informal approaches failed to deal with absenteeism, women's working hours were adjusted so they could better combine the dual roles of mother and worker.

The recruitment of women and the redesign of work around women's responsibilities were seen as emergency measures. The competence of women, and the contribution they made to the war effort, did not trigger a general reassessment of the nature of work. Being bound up with a complex set of social structures, work could not be seen neutrally.

The prevailing character of work had been formed under a patriarchal system, and while the demands of war might cause temporary and partial amendments to the script, the traditional, habitual model was not questioned.

The past in the present

> Contemporary work embodies lineages of a past: work today is not a prisoner of the past but its bruised descendant.[2]

Every institution, every habit and every feature of what we think of as normality has evolved. We are born into a world that has already been shaped. Change continues to modify the social reality we inhabit, but humanity never has the option to start again with a clean sheet. And while social reality has been constructed and modified by the actions of people, it is not a coherent, intentional design. It's the result of uncountable conflicts, arbitrary decisions and mistakes. The ideas of philosophers, religious leaders and kings can be made out amid the noise, but the majority of the culture we inherit is the outcome of complex forces. These are the hardest features of the human landscape to change.

Grint's expression of this truth emphasises that work is something that inhabits us rather than encloses us. Every one of us carries the past within us. We can't shrug this off or wish it away. But, as we will see, it's possible to transcend it.

Beliefs about fundamental differences between men and women remained narrow and fixed for many centuries. The words of a small number of classical authorities were taken as gospel truth. For example, the physician Galen, who had actually been worshipped as a god, advised that women were inferior to men because they are colder. Men used up their heat but women did not, which is why they menstruated and did not go bald (men's energy burned up their hair). Women harboured wandering wombs and were thoroughly damp, making them prone to hysteria and "the vapours".[7]

According to Aristotle, "nature has distinguished between the female and the slave". He reasoned that, since slaves were also men, they could also have "virtue". (In this context, virtue means something like consciousness, rationality or intelligence. However, the word itself derives from the Latin *virtus*, meaning manliness.) Women and children might also have virtue, even though they are not men. But slaves, women and children have different degrees of virtue. For example, a slave has no ability to deliberate, while a women has the ability but not the authority, and the child's deliberative faculty is immature.

We would see the differences between the deliberative ability of slaves and women to be constituted in their power relationships with (free) men. It is hard to see how a lack of authority is naturally endowed, rather than a consequence of social relations. For Aristotle, however, large parts of the social world are taken to be natural, not man-made. Aristotelians believed that as man was perfect then women were imperfect males, were monstrous and were to be ruled by men.[7]

Aristotle can perhaps be forgiven for believing that the normal state of affairs in his time and place represented the timeless, natural order of things. We all automatically use our own situation as the reference point for normality. Aristotle famously believed that women had fewer teeth than men, but this may be because the women he knew did have fewer teeth – from losses due to dietary deficiency. (Even so, you would think he might have taken the trouble to count.) It's the use of authorities such as Aristotle, hardened into ideology, that come to distort objective views of reality.

Like Aristotle, we can mistake practice for law. Just as a slave will seem to have no ability to make free choices, so women will seem to be less intelligent when they are denied access to education. The reason that women have been restricted in their education is because it would be wasted on them because they are less intelligent; a classic example, if ever there was one, of a self-fulfilling prophecy in action. Men will seem to be better at stockbroking when women are barred from stockbroking. The idea that women can't be stockbrokers because they're no good at it is then a circular argument.

Philosophers and theologians, in trying to understand how the universe was structured, created hierarchies. Thomas Aquinas in the thirteenth century had a hierarchy of professions with agriculture at the top, then trades and crafts, with commerce at the bottom.[1] Aquinas also saw women as inferior, as he says in *Summa Theologica*: "Woman is naturally subject to man, because man in man is the discretion of reason."[7]

Luther followed Aquinas in this respect. He believed that women were lower than men in the grand scheme of things and that, compared to men, they were:

- Less rational

- More easily led astray

- More talkative ("from which their husbands and fathers should dissuade them")

- More gregarious

- Less capable of higher development

- Lower in reasoning ability

- Less capable in science and maths.

(Actually, we made the last one up – that was Larry Summers, former president of Harvard University, speaking in 2005.)

For Luther, the size of women's hips in relation to their skulls showed that their primary purpose was childbirth and not thinking.[7]

These views of the different qualities of men and women affected academics' thinking too. Emil Durkheim and Edward Thorndike, the pioneers of sociology and psychology respectively, reached similar conclusions about the abilities of women. Durkheim, a Frenchman from Paris, had concluded, via research on skull sizes, that while the highest level of human evolution could be witnessed, rather handily, in Parisian men, women, even French women, were far less intellectually endowed.[7] Thorndike did not believe that women would ever achieve the greatness of men in areas such as engineering and science.[15]

Humans have a preference for natural explanations. It is simpler to ascribe the ways things are to the design of a god, or the blind process of evolution, than to question the broad distinctions and rules of thumb that guide everyday life. It's easier, safer and more rewarding to conform to the opinions, values and customs of your group than to question them. Offloading the shared worldview on to a deity or entity labelled "nature" is an effective means of denying responsibility for the way things are, and the way they should be.

Such arguments are surprisingly persistent, considering their lack of logic. In a debate with Elizabeth Spelke to discuss Larry Summers's comments, Harvard professor Steven Pinker said that, because of their different brains, there would be fewer women in science and maths departments at the very highest levels of academia such as Harvard. In one stroke, then, Pinker managed to combine the prejudices of Thorndike and Durkheim with the latter's self-regard.

At a 2012 diversity conference in the City of London, one academic stated confidently that there would never be more than 5% of women in foreign exchange dealing because of their hormones. This is despite the fact that there are already parts of the world where there is a higher percentage of women in these roles.

And yet, what's natural does indeed change over time. Aristotle's acceptance of slavery seems bizarre to modern readers. Similarly, what is "fitting" for men and women undergoes continual change. At present, the idea that women should have careers seems to be becoming orthodoxy. We may be at an inflection point where one assumption about "the place" of women is being replaced by its opposite.

The deeply embedded nature of the work ethic was first appreciated following a famous series of experiments carried out at Western Electric's Hawthorne plant in Chicago. The experiments were designed to discover whether different light levels affected workers' productivity. Analysing the confusing results some years later, Henry Landsberger concluded that productivity improved during the experiments simply because the workers knew they were being observed. "Organizations are not machine-like constructs; they are social systems,"

Landsberger found.[16]

The Hawthorne effect tells us that psychologists cannot discount themselves from the social situations they study. More importantly, it tells us that people have a normative attitude to work. That is, people have internalised a set of standards regarding correct behaviour related to the work situation. They know instinctively what they "ought" to be doing, and being observed by someone in a position of authority or higher status reminds them of this knowledge.

Official codes of conduct are no match for deeply held attitudes – attitudes engrained so deeply that we don't even know we hold them. Organisations command our attention, exert authority over our actions and operate reward and sanction systems which aim to circumscribe our behaviour. But they cannot override the effects of socialisation or erase the wider culture in which the organisation is situated. People know that it's wrong to cheat, even when nobody's looking.

Our moral touchstones appear timeless and universal, but they can in fact be artificial and alien. Time and usage have cemented certain beliefs about gender into our psyches to the extent that we perceive them as naturally endowed. And "there is," as Marx argued, "no greater power than when what is actually a sectional interest becomes represented and accepted as a universal interest, as common sense."[2]

References

1. Donkin R. *Blood, Sweat and Tears*. Texere Publishing; 2001.

2. Grint K. *The Sociology of Work*. Polity; 2005.

3. Rose M. *Re-working the Work Ethic*. Batsford Academic and Educational; 1985.

4. Bernstein P. *American Work Values*. SUNY Press; 1997.

5. Nicholson N. *Managing the Human Animal*. Texere Publishing; 2000.

6. Baxandall RF. *America's Working Women*. Vintage; 1976.

7. Wiesner-Hanks ME. *Gender in History*. Wiley-Blackwell; 2011.

8. Morris D. *The Naked Woman*. Random House; 2011.

9. Available at: http://www.theguardian.com/commentisfree/2013/mar/17/mothers-give-me-a-god-delusion. Accessed 19 September 2013.

10. Simonton D. *A History of European Women's Work*. Routledge; 2013.

11. Cooper D. *Talleyrand*. Random House; 2011.

12. Walkerdine V, Jimenez L. *Gender, Work and Community After De-Industrialisation*. Palgrave Macmillan; 2012. doi:10.1057/9780230359192.

13. Shenhav YA. *Manufacturing Rationality*. Oxford University Press; 2002.

14. Thom D. *Women and Work in Wartime Britain*. I.B. Tauris; 2000.

15. Fine C. *Delusions of Gender*. Icon Books; 2011.

16. Witzel M. *Encyclopedia of History of American Management*. Continuum; 2005.

2
THE MAN-MADE ORGANISATION

The division of labour between the genders today is not the result of "natural" differences between the genders, nor does it represent some sort of fixed order. It is in fact a continuation of very long-standing views about what men and women should be doing at work and at home. Work is not a neutral concept but a value-laden creation, a social construct created and perpetuated by us. This construct has as its core the assumption that men are superior to women – physically, mentally, intellectually. The results of these long-held beliefs can be seen today in the way work is organised and it should be no surprise therefore to find that organisations are structured around the lives of men.

This chapter looks at some of the ways in which this bias manifests itself: the division of work, pay, the way work is carried out, career choices and relationships at work.

Division of work and life

Go into virtually any large corporation and you will see an organisation divided along gender lines. Women will predominate in certain functions and men in others. Rarely will you come across an area with an exact 50:50 split. It is also the case that women will be more highly represented in support roles and men in the more highly regarded functions of the business. Divisions of this kind have occurred throughout history and are not based on skill or competence but status.

The Industrial Revolution led men and women to view work differently and to undertake different roles. As we have seen, prior to the Industrial Revolution, men, women and children worked more cooperatively and flexibly together, interchanging roles and responsibilities as circumstances demanded. Nevertheless, one of the key factors behind today's division of labour was the rise of the guild system in the pre-industrial era.

The guild system was predominantly, but not exclusively, male. Girls were apprentices, but in a smaller number of trades. Females could be apprenticed in 19 trades whereas boys could work in 143 trades. Three-quarters of girls in apprenticeships were involved in textiles. Over 33% of male apprentices were involved in timber and leather. Those trades which had the highest premiums and offered better terms were exclusively male and included millers, grocers, cabinet makers, plumbers and curriers. The guilds held status differences too. For males, having a trade and being an apprentice enhanced their standing, whereas it did little to the status of females. The boys were also trained for a longer period – from 14 to 21 years of age.

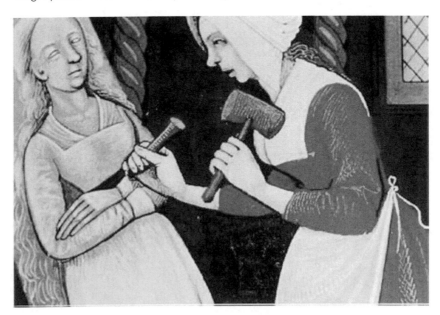

Fig 2.1: Woman sculptor from Boccaccio, Le Livre des Cleres et Nobles Femmes (early 15th century).

The process itself – from apprentice to journeyman to master – reflected a man's lifestyle. Becoming a journeyman entailed travelling and working with different masters, a freedom young women did not have. Having completed an apprenticeship and achieved manhood, it was expected that he would marry and that his wife would then support him in his chosen trade.[1] The man was not only granted freedom of the guild but was expected to enter the public sphere via politics or the local economy. Men's roles therefore encompassed greater education, more expertise and better pay. They were also expected to play out part of their role in the public domain.[2]

Girls, on the other hand, gained no such prestige from their apprenticeships and their lives were destined to be played out in the domestic and private sphere. Marriage was not only her destiny but also the principal route to enhanced status.

Guild work carried prestige and status, as it was skilled, higher quality and better paid. Non-guild work was less skilled, lower quality and more poorly paid. Eventually the work of the guilds came to be seen as honourable work.

There was also a geographical split between where men and women worked and how their work was viewed. Work associated with guilds and men was carried out in towns and was valued more highly to the extent that it was considered to be honourable. Non-guild work consequently was valued less and considered dishonourable and was more likely to be located within the home and in the country. These attitudes towards working from home prevail today. The ribbing that people working from home have to put up with may be good-natured (one of the most common is to put the phrase "working from home" in inverted commas) but it carries distant echoes of what was considered honourable (or dishonourable) work hundreds of years ago.[2]

Table 2.1: Honourable and dishonourable work.

Town	Country
Honourable work	Dishonourable work
Craft	Domestic production
High quality	Low quality
High status	Low status
High pay	Low pay

At the same time, the guilds provided greater work and status opportunities for men and constrained women. Nevertheless women were to be found working in a very wide range of occupations both inside and outside the household. In German markets women would sell produce, in Scotland they brewed beer and across Europe there were female butchers, bakers and innkeepers. The same is true of women settlers in the United States and Canada.[3]

Of course, an important purpose of the guilds was to safeguard the jobs and pay of men. Women were viewed as a danger to both, almost as if they were opportunists and interlopers. It is the case today, as we will see later in this chapter, that women working in typically male areas can find themselves undermined in subtle and not so subtle ways which serve to exclude them.

When looked at from today's perspective, ironies abound. For example, women were not allowed to make dresses as this was considered a guild activity. In France, Prussia and Britain there are recorded instances of women demonstrating about this. Different solutions were arrived at in each region. In England women were allowed to join the dressmaking guilds, while in Prussia women remained blocked from working as dressmakers and, although they were allowed to do so in France, the amount of material they could use was restricted to prevent them from making more elaborate garments.[2] Each of these approaches to the same objections embraces a different view about a woman's abilities from "They can't make dresses" to "They can make dresses but they aren't able to make the more ornate ones" to "They are able to make any dress that a man can". These, then, are emotional and attitudinal obstacles, not matters of skill, capability or motivation.

During the time of the guilds the word "mystery" was used to describe the process of acquiring mastery in a craft. This process was partly about acquiring skills, partly concerned with performing rituals and undergoing rites of passage, and partly about experiencing an enigmatic and unobservable transfer of knowledge. (Skill, at least in France and Britain, also encompassed size and strength, thus serving as another barrier to would-be female entrants.) But "mystery" was also associated with management and leadership, which therefore became a male preserve.

The Industrial Revolution saw the rise of large professional bodies for groups such as engineers, chemists and accountants. All of these jobs required an education and therefore excluded women, who were not allowed into many universities. Although the University of London admitted women from 1877, it was nearly 70 years later in 1946 that the University of Cambridge did the same. In France, the Sorbonne admitted women in 1880 but two other Grandes Ecoles only started to accept women in the 1960s.[2] It was only in the 1960s that Harvard University, Princeton University and New York University allowed women to be granted PhDs. Opportunities for women in the professions were therefore limited or non-existent. But there were jobs to be had in the unskilled work produced by Taylorism, with women replacing men in many countries in Europe and North America because they were cheaper to employ.

In some cases, professionalisation led to the removal of women from jobs they had previously carried out. For example, women had practised medicine in France but after 1755 they were banned from specialist areas, except for midwifery. The dual mechanisms of restricted access and ejection led to all the professions, including medicine, becoming male-dominated. Official professional recognition of the occupations that women predominantly carried out was achieved much later, for example in the case of midwives and nurses. Formal training and education was not considered necessary for these occupations as it was felt that women would learn best from other women who were already carrying out the role. Yet, bizarre as it may seem now, the best midwives were considered to be men as they had received a higher education and consequently were paid more.[2]

As well as nursing and midwifery, the other types of work available to women related to their domestic roles – cooking, caring and cleaning. Anything that supposedly did not require much training or education was deemed suitable for females.

Another pattern seen consistently through history is the way new technology and equipment is at first the possession of men, whether this is the scythe replacing the sickle in Roman times, mechanical weaving during the Industrial Revolution, or computer technology today.[1,2,4] The jobs associated with new equipment are seen, initially at least, as being of higher status, and thus reserved for men. However, once the technology is used to deskill and to lower costs, the same equipment loses its exclusivity and is increasingly used by women. When typewriters were first introduced into the workplace men were to be found using them. It was only later that the secretarial role became viewed as quintessentially female.[3] Later still the keyboard was the primary tool for computing. This is designated as science and has been seen as a male profession.[1]

The Industrial Revolution also led to a very different conceptualisation of what a woman's role should be. In France, Jules Simon asked, "What is a man's vocation? It is to be a good citizen. And a woman's? To be a good wife and a good mother. One is in some way called to the outside world: the other for the interior."[2]

In Britain, similar statements were expressed by John Ruskin: "The man's work for his own home is to secure its maintenance, progress and defence: the woman's is to secure its order, comfort and loveliness."[2]

Charitable and good works represented one area where women could express themselves, although even this was at first disapproved of. Florence Nightingale, in many ways the creator of modern-day nursing, said that "[t]he family is too narrow a field for the development of an immortal spirit, be that spirit male or female".

Women, especially married women, often withdrew from the workplace, which served to increase their dependence on their husbands. The notion of a family workforce was steadily replaced by that of the sole male breadwinner, thereby helping to create a model for men's and women's working patterns which is still with us. The men in turn were dependent on their wives to enable them to provide for the household. The increased mutual dependency leads to greater prescriptions about the role of each gender: this is what women do and this is what men do. The safeguarding and patrolling of these borders is then an essential activity to maintain the status quo and keep men in the high-status position, and is present in the workplace and society today.

But throughout history we see many examples of women successfully undertaking roles that were seen as men's. The First and Second World Wars both saw millions of women engaging in tasks that were once seen as the preserve of men. This led, albeit temporarily, to changing long-established workforce practices. During the First World War, women were paid the same wages as men. This was not due to a sense of equality but an anxiety that men's jobs would be at risk if employers could see that the same work could be carried out for less money by women.[5] During the Second World War, as we noted in Chapter 1, workplace nurseries for preschool children were introduced on a large scale and there was greater flexibility to allow women to shop for provisions and to carry out domestic work. When the war ended so did these practices.[6] But at other times too, for example when men were away due to the seasonal nature of their work, women would take charge of affairs. In other words, women's skills are acknowledged when a situation calls for it, but it is time-bounded and temporary. Women can stand in for men temporarily, but business returns to normal when men can be found.

Career choices

Women's career choices are more limited and more restricted than men's, which is both the cause and the effect of the gendered division of roles that we see playing out in today's workforce. This division has an impact on the career choices of boys and girls from an early age. If a child sees certain roles being carried out by one gender or another, this will have an influence on the child's occupational choices. Children learn from a young age the gender of the person they expect to be carrying out certain roles. Since work is such an important part of our lives, these observations and decisions are critical for our subsequent life paths.

When we look at girls' and women's occupational and life choices we see that they have always been constrained. In seventeenth-century Germany, France and Britain, girls were expected to work harder than boys and from an earlier age, and they were trained at an earlier age in domestic skills.

In the seventeenth century, there were a number of routes to adulthood.[2]

Years	A	B	C	D	E
Birth	Home	Home	Home	Home	Home
7			School	School	Work (Depending on class)
10	Parish apprenticeship				
14		Private apprenticeship	Private apprenticeship	Work/service	Work/home
21	Work	Work			
23.5-24.5	← Females: Marriage, child-rearing →				
25.5	← Males: Marriage →				

Boys were represented in all five patterns but girls were in A, D and E, the majority being in pattern E.

To be fulfilled in a career means that the work being carried out is suited to an individual's personality and motivation. As such, career choices involve knowing about the area of work but also about ourselves – our interests, activities and aspirations.

Vocational psychologist Linda Gottfriedson has been particularly influential in this area. In her theory of circumscription and compromise, Gottfriedson[7] argues that our vocational choices are influenced not only by our personalities but also by societal values and the roles we see people carrying out around us. Gender and desirability of the occupation play a key part in our choices. While our personalities are at least in part inherited, our ideas and values associated with each vocation are culturally determined. As a society, we have determined what value to assign to any given role and whether we see it as male or female.

Our biology and our knowledge of different career choices leads us to find appropriate jobs, a behaviour known as niche seeking. Circumscription involves narrowing down our choices, eliminating those that do not fit with our self-image and social identity and following those that do.

Children receive messages from an early age about what are – and are not – acceptable occupations for someone of their gender and social class. This is not a conscious process: these messages are absorbed via all of the daily influences around us – parents, teachers, friends and the media.

By the age of 13, Gottfriedson says, children will start to eliminate, albeit unconsciously, jobs that are "inappropriate for one's sex". Then occupations are ruled out because of prestige. Finally they consider the effort that needs to go into getting into the profession. From this point, the matching process becomes more conscious and other factors may come into play. For many boys a key factor will be earning significant income to provide for the family, whereas girls may focus on how to balance work and future family demands. These issues become important considerations in determining vocational and career choice. Young people's choices begin to form around what appears to be realistic and achievable.

Circumspection, then, in many ways is about the messages girls and boys receive about what is an acceptable direction to take. Compromise involves, within the careers they opt for, giving up their most preferred choices in favour of something they feel is more attainable.

The criteria for deciding which roles are most accessible are sex type, prestige and field of work. Girls' choices are constrained to a greater extent than boys' choices, however, because many high-prestige roles such as engineer, scientist or surgeon are deemed to be male. Other vocations such as lawyer or accountant are proving to be less sex-typed, but leadership positions in these professions certainly are. Other roles such as nursing and teaching are commonly seen as female roles, and have lower prestige. We would argue that this is not because they are inherently of less worth. It is rather that such roles have lower status *because* they are associated with women.

In a study[8] examining gender preferences in a sample of half a million people, using Holland's vocational type theory, it was found that men showed stronger preference for (using Holland's labels):

- Realistic roles: activities involving working with tools, machines, animals. Types of job included mechanic, farmer and electrician

- Investigative roles: examination of physical, biological or other scientific phenomena, e.g. scientist, engineer.

Women showed stronger preferences for:

- Conventional roles: those that are rule-regulated, involving record keeping and administration, e.g. accountancy, auditing, secretarial work, office/ administrative work

- Social roles: working with others, teaching, developing and helping others, e.g. teacher, counsellor or nurse

- Artistic roles: creating art forms or products, e.g. painter, sculptor, designer, writer.

It has been argued that these preferences reflect genuine, innate differences in personality between the genders. Yet in eighteenth-century Europe, while there were no girls in apprenticeships in Germany, 9% of girls in England and 19% of girls in Geneva were in apprenticeships.[2] This situation has worsened over the years, to such an extent that only 2.6% of trade jobs in the United States today are held by a women. Societal pressures and subtle (and sometimes not so subtle) indoctrination persuades young people what suitable occupations are for each gender.

But of course it is not just girls who are making career choices. Boys make decisions that are not just masculine but anti-feminine, as represented by jobs that stereotypically appear to need toughness and emotional restrictiveness.[9] In that case women in such roles will seem even more like intruders.

A fascinating longitudinal study[10] of more than 1,000 people over a forty-year period showed that while personality clearly played a part in occupational choice, so too did socialisation and stereotyping. Those who were assessed as high on the personality dimension of openness, which includes imagination and curiosity, were less likely to go into gender-stereotypical roles, than those assessed as low on the same dimension. Such children were more likely to be able to visualise themselves carrying out less typical roles and as a consequence they developed less stereotypical interests as they grew older. Other studies have shown that girls aged as young as two to three aspire to gender-stereotypic roles. Girls choosing non-stereotypic roles were less likely to persist in their choices.[11,12]

In the past the obstacles to pursuing non-stereotypical careers were overt and obvious. Societal disapproval would have been explicit and the penalties clear. Today, the barriers are not so obvious, as they are related to attitudes and perceptions, but they are no less real because of this. The gender typing of roles and professions will continue because of the circularity of the argument: these are jobs that someone of my gender does and so these are the ones that I will consider.

The pay gap

Economists have pored over remuneration data for very large cohorts in Britain and, although gender pay gaps were clearly evident, they had to conclude with mild frustration that the reasons for this imbalance "remain in a way unexplained".[13] This puzzling inexplicability could be interpreted as their failing to see a rational reason why gender pay gaps exist. The reason an explanation eludes them is simply that the cause is not rational but emotional. The phenomenon of unequal pay is not rooted in *facts* about work, but in *beliefs* about the inherent value of men and women at work. One of the reasons, whether explicitly acknowledged or not, why women are excluded from the higher-paid crafts and trades and from leadership positions in organisations is that allowing them in would lead to remuneration levels falling.

Another reason why a pay gap exists – and such gaps exist in all major economies – is because of the role expectations we have of men and women. Men are meant to provide and women are meant to be supported: providing equal pay would distract them from this role. Yet this view of gender roles only emerged in the eighteenth and nineteenth centuries, and gender pay gaps existed long before this.

The earliest advice on pay is to be found in the Bible in Leviticus – the same Leviticus who frowned upon gay relationships (and who also, although this is rather less well known, abhorred people wearing cotton and linen together!). Leviticus says: "Set the value of a male between the ages of twenty and sixty at fifty shekels of silver according to the sanctuary shekel; for a female, set the value at thirty shekels; for a person between the ages of five and twenty set the value of a male at twenty shekels and of a female at ten shekels." So a female's pay, according to Leviticus, should be 50–60% that of a male's. This was written two to three thousand years ago yet throughout history, where records are available, it is remarkable to see how faithfully these ratios are reflected in actual pay rates. In the sixteenth century, for example, women in Europe received 52–61% of men's earnings.[6] In nineteenth-century Europe, women earned between 33% and 66% of men's pay.[2]

There have been exceptions to this basic rule established by our biblical prophet. After the Black Death in the fourteenth century, women reapers were paid the same as men.[4] In the early seventeenth century women earned 90% of men's pay, but eighty years later this had fallen back to just above what Leviticus advised, at 67%.[2]

The gender pay gaps we see in many countries today are not as bad as they have been historically. But this doesn't make them fair.

Some economists have argued that men were paid more in earlier times because when greater muscle power was required, men could get more done using their greater physical strength.[13] However, this falls into the classic trap of assuming that all men are stronger than all women, which is clearly not the case. The introduction of the corn scythe to replace the sickle, for example, saw only men using the new tool, even though women were, when given the opportunity, just as skilled at using it. This is a clear example of a new tool being utilised by the higher-status group.

Nevertheless, the gender pay gap has certainly diminished. During the First World War, as mentioned above, women in Britain had to take on many of the roles previously performed by men. A special Act of Parliament was passed to allow this to happen, and women were paid the same as men while the war continued. The work for both genders was demanding and unrelenting, but this period proved to be a significant turning point in terms of greater acceptance of working women and their capabilities.[5]

During the Industrial Revolution the perception of a woman's role changed. This is encapsulated in the verdict of Andrew Ure (1778–1857), an enthusiastic re-animator of corpses (the real-life inspiration for *Frankenstein*) and self-appointed propagandist for the joys of work in mill and mine. Ure saw the purpose of industry being purely to maximise profits and one way of doing this was to keep costs down. Fewer people in the higher wage categories should be employed, meaning more people in the 11–16 age category and fewer in the 16–21 band. For those above 21, he suggests, "only those men will be employed who are necessary to do the work requiring great bodily strength, or great skill, in some art or craft, or mystery in which they are employed in office of trust and confidence".[14] It is men who are able to undertake these roles.

Ure criticised those who were concerned about the low wages paid to women "since the low price of their labour here tends to make household duties their most profitable as well as agreeable occupation and prevents them from being tempted by the mill to abandon their offspring at home." With a grand flourish he declares: "Thus Providence effects its purposes with a wisdom and efficacy which should repress the short-sighted presumption of human devices." Women are therefore to be paid less precisely because of the need for them to concentrate on their domestic duties, which form their true purpose and mission in life![14]

Employers chose not to follow Ure's advice, but in a way that he would have found congenial. Greater industrialisation meant many jobs becoming less skilled, so more women were taken on by employers because they were cheaper and could be laid off more easily. Even in those days women were seen as more "flexible" – meaning expendable.

The persistent drive to get women out of certain types of work in the nineteenth century led to married women becoming more dependent on their husbands. The trend also undermined single women. Today, women around the world remain in jobs that are associated with low status and low income. The gender pay gap is attributed to a variety of reasons:[15]

- Women being less qualified
- Occupational sex segregation (women are to be found in the lower-paid roles and professions)
- Women being mothers
- The number of women in part-time employment
- Women taking on the role of carer and men that of breadwinner
- Ethnicity.

Research in the United States has stated that 40% of the gender gap is due to unexplained reasons including sex discrimination.[16] (Other research has estimated that 29% of the pay gap is due to overt or unconscious discrimination.[17])

The gap exists among lower-paid women, highly skilled and high-earning professionals, unmarried women and women without children and exists in all European and Western countries. In Denmark, over a ten-year period from 1996 to 2005, female senior executives earned 69% of a male's salary when all other factors are controlled for.[18] In Britain, for example, when factors such as age, social class, geography, education and children were controlled for, women born in 1958 earned about 35% less than men born in the same year.[19] According to the Organisation for Economic Co-operation and Development (OECD), there is a 19% gender pay gap in the United States, although some more recent research places this much higher.[16]

Women with children fare worse than those without children, and women working part-time fare even worse than women working full-time. This has been seen as possibly due to organisations deciding that women working part-time may not be as productive. There is no evidence to suggest that this is the case, which means that we are once again dealing with an irrational or emotional response to women working part-time. Women themselves appear to accept that working part-time will indeed lead to reduced income because they see part-time working as a job-related benefit.[13] This "benefit" clearly operates in a very different way from other benefits, which are seen as *adding* to your income, not taking from it.

The cohort studies of British women concluded that "when all else is held constant, motherhood does not appear to lead to one woman being much worse paid than another with no children." However, working part-time did lead to lower incomes, as did taking an extended period of maternity leave. The pay gap was "more severe for mothers who have full-time jobs but a broken employment record at the time of the first birth".[13]

The effect of gender on pay has been measured with some precision. In one experiment, 127 professors at American universities agreed to evaluate a CV to determine a candidate's suitability for a role as a laboratory manager.[20] They were asked to assess the candidate's competence on a scale of 1 to 7 and to recommend a starting salary. However, deploying one of the sneaky tricks loved by experimental psychologists, all the academics were sent the same CV, but with the names altered. For half of the sample, the candidate was called John, and for the other half Jennifer. On competence, John received an average score of 4 to Jennifer's 3.3. John was offered an average starting salary of $30,328 and Jennifer $26,508. In other words, employers were prepared to pay a 14% premium simply to employ a man. Intriguingly, the female professors displayed the same bias as the male.

The gender pay gap has huge implications for savings, pensions and financial and psychological independence. In the World Economic Forum (WEF)'s Corporate Gender Gap Report,[21] a survey covering more than 20 countries, 16 industries and some of the world's largest corporations, only 28% of the companies track gender salary gaps. Just over half of the companies that do not track this data believe that it is unnecessary, as they do not believe that the gender pay gap exists in any case; a policy that is best called "burying your head in the sand".

One response to today's risibly named "War for Talent"[22] is the increase in salaries of leaders in our major corporations. These people, leaders – men, in other words – command their great salaries because their skills are rare. Of course, if women were considered equally capable of doing these jobs, then the size of the available labour market would double – the War for Talent could perhaps then be downgraded to a tiff.

One response to this is that women should negotiate harder for more pay, but this is easier said than done for two reasons. First, women tend to compare their own pay to that of other women[23] and, second, when they do negotiate for more money, they are treated more harshly than men.[24] There are greater penalties, therefore, for being seen to be non-compliant.

Women are paid less than men at all levels – in spite of legislation in many countries making this illegal. So, that being the case, if you want a business case for diversity, how about this one: *increase profits instantly by replacing your very expensive senior management with less expensive female talent.* We are not saying that you should pay women less, nor are we saying that men should have their salaries cut. What we are saying is that, given that women have the same leadership capabilities and potential as men (as we explain in more detail in Chapter 5), why don't companies take advantage of this situation to reduce costs and increase profits at a stroke?

The gender pay gap is, of course, unfair. It is the most glaringly obvious unfairness that exists in our society. There is no business case for closing the gap because doing so will make an immediate and sustained dent in a company's profits. If ever there was a reason for questioning the business case for diversity, surely this is it. The decision at stake here is not a business one, but a moral one.

Work and flexibility

Work is conducted in certain regulated patterns at particular times and places. Outside these constraints we have a life – or so the expression "work–life balance" would have us believe.

In most circumstances the "ideal" is for work to be carried out in the workplace, full-time. Despite the statements organisations make and the policies they write, in our experience anything that varies from this is not just *different* from the norm, but *worse*. This includes working flexibly, working from home, job sharing and especially part-time working.

Policies enabling working patterns of this kind may appear to be applicable to both men and women, but their development and implementation are highly gendered. It is fashionable to describe policies enabling such working patterns as "family-friendly". The assumption contained in the expression is important and significant: the most acceptable reason to work flexibly is for family.

The reason for having such policies was to retain women in an organisation. You don't have to be a genius to see that flexible working is clearly aimed at, and linked to, working mothers. Society expects men to be the breadwinners and women to look after the family and the household generally. However, because of their association with women, family and domestic work are seen as less productive and less worthwhile, and as not being "real" work. These practices are denigrated even while organisations congratulate themselves for introducing ways of accommodating them.

Don't misunderstand us: we are not saying that such policies are wrong. They are exactly what is needed in today's workplace. It is the way we view such policies that is problematic.

Organisations increasingly expect their employees not only to do a good job, but to identify with the brand. They must not only understand customers but be consumers themselves: to sell the brand at every opportunity and to act as ambassadors for the company. This was not always the case. When the term "greedy institutions" was coined in the 1970s it referred to monastic life and military organisations that expected to own you body and soul. These organisations put pressure on their members "to weaken their ties or not to form any ties with other institutions or persons that might make claims that conflict with their own demands".[25] Coser observed that such organisations:

> Tend to rely on voluntary compliance and to evolve means of activating loyalty and commitment. The monk or the bolshevik, the fascist or the sectarian have chosen a way of life in which they engage themselves totally, even though they may be subject to rigid social controls, and most women accept the mandate of completely committing themselves to their families. Greedy institutions aim at maximising assent to their style of life by appearing highly desirable to the participants.[25]

Today's new generation of companies based on disseminating information and knowledge have been compared to the monasteries of the Middle Ages.[26] However, they also demand total dedication not just to the job but to the aims and aspirations of the corporation itself. Anything which demonstrates a lack of devotion or commitment will be treated with suspicion and as a result will be viewed negatively. This is how flexible working is seen: it is a deviation from the norm and is for the individual's benefit, not that of the organisation. It is a selfish act in contrast to the selflessness displayed by everyone else, who turn up at work every day to put in a shift for the organisation and for their team mates.

This way of working – full-time, at the workplace – is a model that suits men and fits in with the breadwinner role established in the nineteenth century. But becoming a working parent does not just create work–life balance problems; it creates work–life conflict. Society places different expectations on mothers and fathers. We expect a father, implicitly and explicitly, to be the breadwinner, providing the means to support his family. A good mother is available for the children at all times.[27] These roles have become accepted as "the way things are" but, as we have seen, this was not the case before the Industrial Revolution. The result is that mothers at work experience greater work–life conflict than fathers do.

Psychologists are by no means innocent bystanders in all this. John Bowlby's theory of attachment was used as a tool in the reassignment of women to the home after the relative freedom of the Second World War. Attachment theory claims that a child and his primary caregiver, who is by and large the mother, build "a warm, intimate, and continuous relationship"[28] from the moment of birth. Failure to develop a secure and unambiguous attachment is thought to lead to behavioural and emotional problems in the child throughout their life. Attachment is different from bonding, in that both mother and child are involved, and it is not hormonally triggered.

Attachment theory can therefore be used to bolster the idea that women should stay at home with their children. If women don't produce securely attached children, then they are responsible for creating delinquents and depressives. Despite being differentiated from the age-old idea of bonding, attachment is still a somewhat mystical process – just the kind of duty likely to create maximum guilt and anxiety on the part of mothers:

> There has been the occasional "expert" over the years who has decreed that if you do not stare into your baby's eyes non-stop for the entire first year of its life, eventually you will be punished for it by ending up with a stupid, miserable child. Clearly, this is complete balls.[29]

In common with the majority of psychological theories, attachment theory assumes the mother is the only parent who counts. Failing to develop attachment between a baby and its father, or other caregivers, seems not to matter. Whatever its primary intentions, Bowlby's theory can be used to spray a scientific sheen on the prescriptive allocation of women to home and hearth. Theories in this area are often classed under the damning label of "maternal deprivation". However, one of the most notable ways in which humans differ from other primates is the extent to which both parents share in the care of their offspring. The offloading onto the mother the care of children is therefore actually not natural at all.

We are all conflicted about the roles we should take in society. Women want a career, but they know they "should" be at home. Not only is it impossible for women to "have it all", it's inevitable that they will feel as if they are failing at everything. Men don't necessarily want to be breadwinners, but feel less than men if they do not provide for their family. Men worry about how they will be viewed if they opt to stay at home and look after their children – not just by other men, but by the mothers they'll meet at toddler groups. The gender divide is done to us, but we also do it to ourselves. We rigorously police the status quo with regard to our own attitudes and choices.

The models that underpin these dilemmas are quite explicit. In these conflicted situations, each actor is trying to be a good parent and a good citizen. But what it means to be a good parent or citizen differs depending on whether you are a man or a woman.

The creation of flexible work policies is a way of addressing this issue, but the way we view such policies merely reinforces the stereotypical roles we believe men and women should fulfil. Working flexibly, and in particular part-time, entails taking risks with your career and your remuneration. Such policies can work in very contradictory ways – both to enhance and reduce opportunities for women.[15] They enable women to manage their work and home commitments, rather than challenging the balance of responsibilities between the two partners. This solution enables both partners to maintain their prescribed roles in society:

the woman can spend more time in the home and the man's role is not changed or challenged at all.

By choosing to work flexibly, individuals will be seen as "time deviant".[30] The consequences for time deviancy are serious, the most significant being that you cannot take this path and expect to fulfil your career ambitions. Working flexibly will mean becoming disconnected from your career. And this will favour men for senior roles in organisations.

Men are seen as unencumbered, without any external responsibilities or distractions that could interfere with management activity. But because women are seen to have, or indeed are expected to have, responsibilities outside the workplace, their capabilities and commitment will be questioned, which in turn can lead women to question whether senior positions are even attainable to them.[31] The double standard at play here can be seen on those (rare) occasions when a male employee confesses to being late or unavailable due to a childcare commitment. He will probably be admired for this act of heroism. However, he should be careful not to show too much of his "feminine" side. Global research carried out by the World Economic Forum revealed that when women took extended maternity leave only 54% returned to the same level of management or higher. For men the figure was an even more measly 46%. It appears that men are penalised more for taking long-term parental leave. Men's doubts about taking up these options therefore appear to have some foundation.

Part-time working adds another layer of disadvantage on women. Sixty per cent of working mothers who work part-time are in four occupational categories:

- Elementary administration or service
- Sales and customer service
- Caring personal service
- Administrative.[32]

Only 3% of mothers working part-time are corporate managers. It would seem, therefore, that part-time working is simply incompatible with management.[32] Furthermore, those working part-time are seen as less committed and producers of lower-quality work. They receive less training and are seen as having fewer job prospects.[33]

However, not all part-time work is the same.[34] There is another category of part-time working, sometimes referred to as retention, where someone who is recruited to a full-time role is subsequently granted part-time working. Here the person will have volunteered or requested to change work patterns; they will typically be more skilled and their career prospects will be better.

Since, as we have seen from the pay studies, working part-time is seen as a benefit, those employed under these arrangements can feel trapped in an organisation because they believe they will be unable to get the same working arrangements elsewhere.

Professionals and managers experience part-time work differently. Professionals have greater autonomy but those in managerial roles work longer hours, with less autonomy – they are, in effect, required to fit with the male model of working, which in turn leads to greater frustration with factors such as promotion prospects, lack of challenge and variety, and being underutilised in their roles.

The gendered nature of flexible working reveals itself further, however, when we realise that more men would like to work flexibly than ask for it. One of the key reasons for this, notes psychologist Jennifer Whelan, "is that working flexibly is stereotypically seen to show a lack of ambition or commitment."

When men elect to work part-time this usually occurs later in their careers, when they are nearing retirement or are well enough established in their roles that their status would not be diminished. If part-time working occurs earlier in a male's career it will be due to involuntary reasons such as studying or being made redundant, or to enhance their breadwinner role by taking on another job. Nevertheless a high proportion of men are, and probably will continue to be, involved in caring duties. One study showed that 33% of employees with caring responsibilities are male, the majority of whom were looking after their spouses.[6]

In many organisations with which the authors have worked, the experience of part-time workers is noticeably worse than that of those working full-time. Part-timers are less likely to be promoted, paid bonuses, trained or even have their performance appraised. Although this has an impact on all those working part-time, regardless of whether they are male or female, it is untrue to say that this is not a gender issue. The majority of people working part-time are female, and it is for that reason that it becomes a gender issue.

The dual role of jobs and family for women means that they work, in overall terms, longer hours than men. You don't often think of statisticians as being cheeky, but we like to think that Britain's Office for National Statistics decided to cause a few ripples when they calculated that if domestic work was paid for at the average hourly rate it would represent 122% of the work carried out in the paid economy.[6] By any analysis, that is a lot of work.

Women's involvement in paid employment has been increasing significantly since the 1960s. However, the gap in domestic division of labour (DDL) is changing much more slowly.[35] While the gap between men and women in terms of DDL has reduced, this is primarily due to women doing less housework rather than men doing more. Research in this area also reveals the gap between attitude and behaviour. Men in different countries espouse different attitudes regarding their roles and those of women. But in terms of actual work being done, there is hardly any difference between those holding conservative or more liberal views. What we have seen, therefore, over the past few decades is a change in attitude but not in behaviour.

This may be because the pressures on men not to change are simply too great. Working long hours, the expectation of much higher commitment, and the identification of the individual with the goals of the organisation all contribute to some people being less able to participate fully in domestic duties. Of course, it also works out to a man's advantage to have someone taking care of all that other stuff.

While the "work" part of "work–life balance" has been more constrained for women, so has the "life" part. In the past, certain activities were permissible to women but not others including writing and music. Female authors regularly adopted male pseudonyms. Without formal education it was difficult for women to read music and play instruments – a situation that only started to change once the manufacture of pianos for the home began. Conversations about social life became divided by gender, but not because women can't be interested in sport, for example, but because social activities were prescribed.

It is often assumed that women are not interested in sport because they are, well, women. Take football in England. This is a pastime and a career pursued mainly by men and watched by men. But this was not always the case. Indeed, working-class men used actively to support women's football matches. In 1895, women's football matches regularly attracted crowds of 10,000. (As points of comparison, the first FA Cup Final drew a crowd of 37,000 and the FA Amateur Cup Final 7,000.)

Women managed to participate in football despite having to work a "double day" – long shifts followed by domestic duties. As the sport's popularity increased among women, so did the debate about the appropriateness of their involvement and whether it was "natural" for them. But the female players enjoyed the experience:

> Women had blocks of leisure time that had been "earned" in public, sufficient for colleagues to form teams and access to resources like pitches that would otherwise not have been made available. Work and leisure for female players... were fused.[36]

The peak of women's football during this period was 26 December 1920 at Everton's Goodison Park ground in Liverpool, when a crowd of 55,000 paid to watch a women's match (it was estimated that up to 15,000 more spectators were locked out). The appeal of women's football became a matter of concern

Fig 2.2: Women's football, 26 December 1920, Goodison Park, Liverpool.

for the authorities at the Football Association who in their wisdom, less than a year later, on 5 December 1921, adopted the following resolution: "Complaints have been made as to football being played by women, the council feel impelled to express their strong opinion that the game of football is quite unsuitable for females and ought not to be encouraged".[36] Thereafter they decreed that no FA teams could use their grounds for women's matches.

While sport was not seen by the authorities as appropriate for women, shopping was. With the advent of brands in the late nineteenth and early twentieth centuries, organisations saw the opportunity of selling their products to women in the household. The advertising profession which grew alongside the brands sold not just products nor the role that a woman should play in society, but the very idea of shopping itself. Home–work; consumer–breadwinner; shopping–sport; the gendered view of roles creates not just gendered organisations but gendered interests.

This unequal division of domestic work has other consequences apart from creating work–life conflict. It means that women, especially those with families, have less time to socialise after work. They therefore have fewer opportunities to build networks.

Ingroups, outgroups and networks

We all belong to identity groups which can cut across departments, divisions and locations. Externally, such groups include professional associations and unions. But such groupings also exist within organisations.[37] Gender is one of the most easily identifiable identity groups.

Identification with a group can create cohesion – that is, the extent to which a group feels united, or even uniform. Cohesion is a quality that many teams and groups strive to achieve for the benefits it brings, namely increased levels of engagement, closer identification with a group's goals, increased levels of satisfaction, reduced absenteeism and turnover.[37]

These are all very worthwhile aims – which can come at a cost. A team that is too cohesive can become more monotone in its thinking and less willing to tolerate dissent. Such a team is more prone, in other words, to groupthink which occurs where moral judgement "reality testing" is by-passed, particularly in the face of high-risk decisions in high status groups.

Interpersonal cohesion is essentially about team members getting on. This creates a good working environment but can mean that people do not feel able to express themselves and will therefore go along with the group even when they disagree, in order to maintain consensus. This behaviour is a form of self-censorship and at its most extreme groupthink occurs where individuals suspend their sense of what is right and wrong.[38]

Groups not only provide identity to individuals but also support. Networking within organisations enables easy transfer of information and knowledge, which in turn opens up opportunities, provides resources and provides assistance when required. The more powerful a network is, the greater the support provided.

Networking is not just about time at work – importantly, it spills over into so-called leisure time. In fact, it can sometimes be difficult to identify where work ends and leisure begins. External social activities are often crucial in developing, maintaining and nurturing one's network. Women are disadvantaged here in three main ways.

First, the nature of group dynamics, norms and the dominance of men in work means that women are more likely to be excluded from networks. Second, roles that women and men are expected to play at work and home further limit women's abilities to participate in these networks. Third, typically women will have less time to devote to these activities, given the domestic tasks they are required to undertake. These three reasons help us to understand why networks in organisations consistently serve to exclude women. Albeit often unconsciously, some group identities include masculinity as a marker, and certainly for many groups – such as professional, skilled and leadership groups – women have been deliberately excluded over centuries. Being male is so deeply embedded in the identity of many groups that we do not even recognise its existence. (Not if you are a man, at any rate.)

So, networking has itself evolved to be a subtly male preserve. For example, the type of conversations and activities that can bond a group of men together usually involve discussions around sport.

It has been suggested that men exclude women from their networks because they wish to be with those that they feel most sure of.[39] A culture can then be created by men which reflects their interests and concerns, otherwise known as a corporate patriarchy, something identified as a major obstacle to gender equality in the WEF's gender gap report.[21]

In her seminal work *Men and Women of the Corporation*[39] Rosabeth Moss Kanter referred to the use of women as tokens in organisations. This situation occurs where women make up 15% or less of a given population. As tokens, women are:

- More visible
- Under greater scrutiny regarding their performance
- Excluded from informal networks or marginalised.

Intriguingly, a small number of women being present creates ambiguities in terms of group and individual identity, the response to which is to exaggerate the differences between men and women. This in effect raises the boundaries between them – they appear more distinct as groups. It is not surprising that more women leave organisations where they are tokens and have to work under such oppositional conditions. And the self-removal of women then serves to strengthen male bonds and rituals.

Being a token woman amplifies the effects of gender discrimination experienced by non-token women. Research[40] following in Kanter's footsteps, comparing the experience of token women to that of non-tokens, found that the most significant barrier for both tokens and non-tokens was the "men's club". While 47% of non-token women identified an entrenched male network culture as a barrier, 72% of tokens did. Other barriers to women progressing in organisations were sex discrimination, prejudice of colleagues and inflexible working patterns. There are two significant points here: first, the barriers were the same for non-tokens as well as tokens – it was the intensity of the experience that changed; second, the barriers are principally attitudinal and not structural.

Clearly, we need to break out of these patterns, but first we need to acknowledge they exist. Organisations have attempted to combat the Old Boys' Network by setting up women's network groups. However, organisations fail to appreciate that there are different types of networks. Expressive networks are based on trust, closeness and friendship and are a key way of getting social support. Instrumental networks, on the other hand, are about information, knowledge, resources and opportunities.[32] Women's networks, while trying to achieve the latter, are ultimately about the former. The point about instrumental networking is that you have access to power in some shape or form. By being part of the network you increase your own capital and worth – you are part of the ingroup. The women's groups, however, involve outgroup members meeting each other, which is missing the point altogether. Furthermore, many women do not choose to join such networks, which have been seen to be divisive and as having negative associations with "victimhood".

It takes time for someone to become accepted within the ingroup. Relationships begin quite formally but gradually become more emotionally embedded, with a greater sense of trust and commitment developing.[41]

The bonding rituals that exist for many men include, as we have seen, discussing sport. Not all men are interested in sport, but sport is not the only means of excluding women. Jokes and banter can also have an impact, most obviously when such behaviour involves sexual innuendo. Where jokes are focused on vulnerabilities of certain groups, this can lead to the creation of a psychologically unsafe place for certain people. Jokes can also serve as a "loyalty test" for the dominant group. Men who go along with the joke are more accepted. But for women the outcome is less clear-cut. Not joining in with the laughter could lead to negative consequences such as isolation and expulsion. Going along with the joke may allow a woman to pass the test of loyalty, but at the price of tacitly accepting the inferior status of women.[39]

Leaders clearly have a big part to play in creating a culture where people feel included. The relationships a leader develops with team members are a key determinant of that culture. According to leader–member exchange theory, subordinates fall into two categories, ingroups and outgroups, and the relationships that are formed are different for each[41] (see Table 2.2).

Table 2.2: Features of relationships between leader and ingroups/outgroups.

Ingroup members	Outgroup members
High-quality relationship with the leader	Low-quality relationship with the leader
Able to negotiate roles	Little ability to negotiate roles
Leaders don't resort to authority or power to lead	Leader relies on power and authority to influence
Likely to stay	Increased turnover
See themselves as important in the exchange of information, knowledge and support	See relationship as a contractual one
Leaders initiate discussion with them	Leaders seldom talk to them
Discuss performance	Little discussion about effectiveness
Provide tacit support	Little help with difficult work
Discuss personal matters	

A survey of 5,500 women in engineering showed the importance of ingroup–outgroup effects. Women make up 20% of engineering undergraduates but only 11% of practising engineers. The main reason women gave for wanting to leave the profession was the culture of engineering. Women felt that their ideas were not taken as seriously, they were undermined and undervalued. The opposite was the case where women wanted to stay in their chosen line of work. The leader–team member relationship therefore was a critical component in how women felt both about the organisation and their profession.[42]

It was believed that increasing the number of women in a given area would break down the gender ingroup–outgroup dynamics. There is some truth in this, but having more women in a team, department or organisation does not appear in itself to bring about a change in culture or practices. The corporate patriarchy model has the most subtle power and influence. This model is so completely woven into the fabric of organisations that conversations frequently, sometimes inadvertently, exclude women. The focus of attention therefore should not be on women and expecting them to change the culture but instead on leaders themselves to reflect on the nature of the relationships they have with their teams, the networks they have created and the way to create a genuinely inclusive culture.

The search for a business case for gender diversity

Women's position in jobs that have been typically held by men has to be justified and legitimised. In other words, a business case needs to be established. In Britain the Davies Report[43] looked at the under-representation of women on boards. The report concluded by saying that there is nothing but an up-side to the presence of women board members. Businesses do better with more women on the board, whatever way you look at it.

This is great news until you examine the data and find that the report's authors either were not aware of research that contradicted their conclusions or, worse, chose to ignore it. There are much more objective reviews of the diversity literature, most recently produced in Britain[44] and Australia,[45] which show the results to be more ambiguous, contradictory and complex than Davies would have us believe. The research data, in fact, show that sometimes gender diversity improves performance, sometimes it makes no difference to performance and at other times it can lead to a decrease in performance. Some of the conclusions the Davies Report arrived at were shown to be, at best, slapdash and casual, and, at worst, propagandist in their attempt to manipulate popular opinion.

The rationale behind the Davies Report, and other publications like it, is that there are rational reasons why women are under-represented in certain roles and positions. The issue is then supposed to be one of ignorance, which can be fixed simply by giving people the right information. The business case for gender diversity is meant to package and present this information so that organisations can make better decisions.

This line of thought can be traced back to Gary Becker, an economist from the University of Chicago, who wrote an influential and still highly relevant book called *The Economics of Discrimination*.[46] He saw discrimination in many respects as a rational act. If someone has a taste for discrimination "he must act *as if* he were willing to pay something, either directly or in the form of reduced income, to be associated with some persons instead of others". Becker provides an example of discrimination against African Americans. An employer would discriminate because "he erroneously underestimates their economic efficiency. This behaviour is discriminatory not because he is prejudiced against them but because he is ignorant of their true efficiency. Ignorance may be quickly eliminated by the spread of knowledge, while a prejudice (i.e. a preference) is relatively independent of knowledge." Becker acknowledged that prejudice is different from ignorance and as a consequence he held that different approaches are needed, depending on context.

Yet, as far as gender is concerned, notions of prejudice, discrimination and bias are not considered important. The Davies Report makes no reference to discrimination, prejudice or bias in the main body of the text. However, in the specially commissioned research conducted for the Davies Report and buried in the report's Annex, the major reason why women are under-represented in the boardrooms of British listed companies was found to be "bias, prejudice or stereotypical behaviour". The work environment or culture was another major factor, which itself will of course be impacted by bias, prejudice and stereotypes.

Unfortunately, this does not fit with the story people wish to tell about gender at work. The evidence is concealed in order to perpetuate the myth that women are under-represented in many roles because of, in Becker's terms, ignorance. And this ignorance is to be combated by knowledge; specifically, the business case. However, in most organisations the senior roles are held by men. So when we are making the business case for gender diversity we are really making a case for more women in those positions. Having greater numbers of women will not in itself lead to other changes. As we have seen, the underlying attitudes and beliefs, whether explicit or implicit, are so strongly held, by both men and women, that increasing representation in itself will not bring about necessary and lasting changes in culture.

Now, take a look at these names:

Adam Applegarth	Fred Goodwin	Lawrence Fish
Andy Hornby	Fred H Langhammer	Mark Fisher
Andy Kuipers	G Truett Tate	Marsha Johnson Evans
Archie G Kane	George L Miles, Jr.	Marshall A Cohen
Bob Bennett	Gordon Pell	Martin J Sullivan
C Taylor	Guy Whittaker	Martin S Feldstein
Christopher Gent	Helen A Weir	Matt Ridley
Colin Matthew	Henry Kaufman	Michael E Fairey
Dan Watkins	J Eric Daniels	Michael H Sutton
Dave Jones	James F. Orr III	Michael L Ainslie
David Baker	Jo Dawson	Mike Ellis
David L Herzog	John D Macomber	Morris W Offit
Edmund S W Tse	John F Akers	Peter Cummings
Ellen V Futter	Johnny Cameron	Phil Hodkinson
Frank G Zarb	Keith Currie	Philip Gore-Randall
Richard C Holbrooke	Richard S Fuld Jr	Robert B Willumstad
Roger S Berlind	Roland A Hernandez	Stephen F Bollenbach
Stephen L Hammerman	Steven J Bensinger	Terri A Dial
Thomas H Cruikshank	Tom McKillop	Virginia M Rometty

Notice anything? These are the names of people responsible for running some of the most profitable companies ever. One notable feature of the list is that it is overwhelmingly male. The list is a mix of non-executive and executive directors of AIG, Lloyds TSB, RBS and Lehmann Brothers from 2007, one year before those organisations crashed and helped to create the global recession.

Despite the recession arguably being a crisis created by men, no one has ever been asked to justify their places at the top table. We find it inconceivable that, if the list of names had been predominantly female, the very notion of women's competence and capability to run organisations would not be questioned. Christine Lagarde's quip that "if Lehman Brothers had been 'Lehman Sisters', today's economic crisis clearly would look quite different"[47] is off the mark. It's more likely that we'd be in the same mess, but the commentariat would have told us we had it coming. Eyes would have rolled, then heads. Then serious questions would have been raised as to whether women are competent to lead businesses.

The business case for "gender diversity" is essentially an argument for more women in leadership. It is an argument that seeks to justify why women should be afforded equality, but assumes they have no right to occupy leadership positions. The business case seeks to answer the question: women – what's the point? No one ever seeks to ask, never mind answer, the equivalent question for men. In other words, the business case for gender diversity is not only a futile exercise but sexist as well.

Imagine there are two candidates for a job – A and B. Both are good, but B is better. Who do you choose? The answer is obvious. So why, if A is male and B is female, is the worse candidate chosen? This injustice happens all the time and will continue to happen unless we recognise that the reasons for it are not rational. It's not necessarily bad practices that are to blame. Bias, stereotyping and prejudice are significant issues. Pretending they are not simply guarantees the continuance of injustice.

The past in the present

In Chapter 1 we looked at the way work has evolved and how this impacted gender relations. The consequences of actions taken in the past are all too evident in today's organisations. The way work is carried out, who does what, where it is carried out and how people are paid all reflect the fact that organisations are operating to a model designed to fit the lifestyles and roles of men. The very fact that a business case is needed to justify women occupying positions traditionally held by men is another indication of how deeply ingrained the assumption of male supremacy is.

The next chapters look at how historical biases are present and at work in organisations today.

References

1. Wiesner-Hanks ME. *Gender in History.* Wiley-Blackwell; 2011.

2. Simonton D. *A History of European Women's Work.* Routledge; 2013.

3. Baxandall RF. *America's Working Women.* Vintage; 1976.

4. Roberts M. 'Sickles and scythes revisited,' in Lane P, Raven N and Snell K (eds), *Women, Work and Wages in England, 1600–1850.* Boydell and Brewer, pp. 68–101.

5. Braybon G. *Women Workers in the First World War.* Routledge; 2012.

6. Grint K. *The Sociology of Work.* Polity; 2005.

7. Gottfredson LS. 'Circumscription and compromise: A developmental theory of occupational aspirations.' *Journal of Counseling Psychology* 1981; 28(6): 545.

8. Su R, Rounds J, Armstrong PI. 'Men and things, women and people: A meta-analysis of sex differences in interests.' *Psychological Bulletin* 2009; 135(6): 859–884. doi:10.1037/a0017364.

9. Jome LM, Tokar DM. 'Dimensions of masculinity and major choice traditionality.' *Journal of Vocational Behavior* 1998; 52(1): 15–15. doi:10.1006/jvbe.1996.1571.

10. Woods SA, Hampson SE. 'Predicting adult occupational environments from gender and childhood personality traits.' *Journal of Applied Psychology* 2010; 95(6): 1045–1057. doi:10.1037/a0020600.

11. Farmer HS, Wardrop JL, Anderson MZ, Risinger R. 'Women's career choices: Focus on science, math, and technology careers.' *Journal of Counseling Psychology* 1995; 42(2): 155–170. doi:10.1037/0022-0167.42.2.155.

12. Fouad NA. 'Work and vocational psychology: Theory, research, and applications. *Annual Review of Psychology* 2007; 58(1): 543–564. doi:10.114 annurev.psych.58.110405.085713.

13. Joshi H, Paci P. *Unequal Pay for Women and Men: Evidence from the British Birth Cohort Studies.* MIT Press; 2001.

14. Ure A. *The Philosophy of Manufactures.* Charles Knight, 1835. Available at http://archive.org/details/philosophymanuf01uregoog. Accessed 3 October 2013.

15. Smithson J, Lewis S, Cooper C, Dyer J. 'Flexible working and the gender pay gap in the accountancy profession.' *Work, Employment & Society* 2004; 18(1): 115–135. doi:10.1177/0950017004040765.

16. Blau FD, Kahn LM. 'The gender pay gap: Have women gone as far as they can?' *The Academy of Management Perspectives* 2007; 21(1): 7–21.

17. Walby S, Olsen W. *The Impact of Women's Position in the Labour Market on Pay and Implications for UK Productivity.* HM Stationery Office, 2002.

18. Smith N, Smith V, Verne M. 'The gender pay gap in top corporate jobs in Denmark: Glass ceilings, sticky floors or both?' *International Journal of Manpower* 2011; 32(2): 156–177.

19.   Lanning T, Bradley L, Darlington R, Gottfried G. *Great expectations: exploring the promises of gender equality*. IPPR Report, 31 March 2013. London: Institute for Public Policy Research.

20.   Available at: http://www.nytimes.com/2012/09/25/science/bias-persists-against-women-of-science-a-study-says.html. Accessed 20 September 2013.

21.   Zahidi S, Ibarra H. *The corporate gender gap report 2010*. World Economic Forum; 2010.

22.   Michaels E, Handfield-Jones H, Axelrod B. *The War for Talent*. Harvard Business Press; 2001.

23.   Eagly AH, Carli LL. *Through the Labyrinth*. Harvard Business Press; 2007.

24.   Bowles HR, McGinn KL. 'Gender in job negotiations: A two-level game.' *Negotiation Journal* 2008; 24(4): 393–410. doi:10.1111/j.15719979.2008.00194.x.

25.   Coser LA. *Greedy Institutions: Patterns of Undivided Commitment*. Macmillan; 1974,p 6.

26.   Donkin R. *Blood, Sweat and Tears*. Texere Publishing; 2001.

27.   Emslie C, Hunt K. '"Live to work" or "work to live"? A qualitative study of gender and work–life balance among men and women in mid-life.' *Gender, Work & Organization* 2009; 16(1): 151–172.

28.   Bowlby J. *Maternal care and mental health: A report prepared on behalf of the World Health Organization as a contribution to the United Nations programme for the welfare of homeless children*, 2nd edn. Geneva: World Health Organization, 1952, p. 28.

29.   Beauman F. *How to Crack an Egg with One Hand: A pocketbook for the new mother*. Bloomsbury Publishing; 2013.

30.   Epstein CF. *The Part-Time Paradox*. Psychology Press; 1999.

31.   Smithson J, Stokoe EH. 'Discourses of work–life balance: negotiating "gender-blind" terms in organizations.' *Gender, Work & Organization* 2005; 12(2): 147–168.

32.   Durbin S, Tomlinson J. 'Female part-time managers: networks and career mobility.' *Work, Employment & Society* 2011; 24(4): 621–640. doi:10.1177/0950017010380631.

33.   Klein KJ, Berman LM, Dickson MW. 'May I work part-time? An exploration of predicted employer responses to employee requests for part-time work.' *Journal of Vocational Behavior* 2000; 57: 85–101.

34.   Lewis S. '"Family friendly" employment policies: a route to changing organizational culture or playing about at the margins?' *Gender, Work & Organization* 1997; 4(1): 13–23.

35.   Crompton R. 'Attitudes, women's employment and the domestic division of labour: A cross-national analysis in two waves.' *Work, Employment & Society* 2005; 19(2): 213–233. doi:10.1177/0950017005053168.

36.   Williams J. *A Beautiful Game*. Berg; 2007.

37.   Thompson PB, McHugh D. *Work Organisations*. Palgrave Macmillan; 2009.

38.   Janis IL. *Victims of Groupthink*. Houghton Mifflin Harcourt; 1972.

39. Kanter RM. *Men and Women of the Corporation*. Basic Books; 2008.

40. Simpson R. 'Gender mix and organisational fit: How gender imbalance at different levels of the organisation impacts on women managers.' *Women in Management Review* 2000; 15(1): 5–18. doi:10.1108/09649420010310173.

41. Landy FJ, Conte JM. *Work in the 21st Century*. John Wiley & Sons; 2009.

42. Foud NA, Singh R. 'Stemming the tide: why women leave engineering.' Available at: http://studyofwork.com/files/2011/03/NSF_Women-Full-Report-0314.pdf. Accessed 20 September 2013.

43. Women on boards. Department for Business Innovation and Skills report, 2011. BIS/11/745.

44. Available at: https://www.gov.uk/government/uploads/system/uploads/attachment_data/file/49638/the_business_case_for_equality_and_diversity.pdf. Accessed 20 September 2013.

45. Available at: http://www.mbs.edu/facultyresearch/ethicalleadership/Documents/Centre%20for%20Ethical%20Leadership%20-%20Targets%20and%20Quotas.pdf. Accessed 20 September 2013.

46. Becker GS. *The Economics of Discrimination*. University of Chicago Press; 1971.

47. Available at: http://dealbook.nytimes.com/2010/05/11/lagarde-what-if-it-had-been-lehman-sisters/. Accessed 20 September 2013.

3

WHAT ARE WE LIKE?
GENDER STEREOTYPES AT WORK

The world we see around us shapes our attitudes and our attitudes shape the world around us.

Here's an experiment you can do for yourself. It was devised by Gary Blasi[1] and goes like this. Try to imagine, without thinking about any specific gender or race, a baseball player, then a trial lawyer, then a figure skater and finally a US Supreme Court judge. How did you get on?

Now, imagine a carpenter. What colour is her hair?

You may have done a double take at this question. It's highly unlikely the question didn't at least cause you to pause.

When we think about a profession or a trade, we often attach gender to it without being aware that we're doing so. As we have seen in Chapters 1 and 2, the history of the crafts and professions is gendered, so it should be no surprise that our perceptions of a role will be gendered too. If a profession summons up the mental image of a man – in both men and women – then women can be disadvantaged in progressing in that career path. It's a learned, automatic and self-reinforced hurdle towards advancement.

This is what stereotypes do to us. They are used to attach both ourselves and others in certain positions and roles and hold us there. At home they perpetuate the myth that it is only the woman who can provide the care children need, devaluing the vital role played by the man in the home. In the workplace, stereotypes help men advance towards senior roles but hinder the progression of women.

Gender stereotypes fall into two classes: descriptive and prescriptive.[2,3] Descriptive stereotypes describe what women and men are like – the traits each gender is thought to possess. Prescriptive stereotypes concern beliefs about what men and women *should* be like and the differences that *should* exist between them. These are discussed in more detail in the next chapter. In this chapter, we look at what stereotypes are, how they are developed, why they are so accepted, and the damage they do in the workplace.

At this stage it is important that we don't make the mistake of thinking that gender stereotyping is purely a male preserve. Women gender stereotype as much as men do[4-7] and both genders have been shown to use gender stereotypes when making hiring decisions. For example, both have a tendency to hire male applicants for high-status, "male" occupations.[8-10]

Where do stereotypes come from?

The word *stereotype* first appears in French around the beginning of the nineteenth century. It originally referred to a kind of printing plate which was coming into use at the time. To make a stereotype plate, you use ordinary metal type or illustration plates to make up your design, then make a mould – using, for example, papier mâché. You then cast a new plate from this mould. The resulting stereotype plate is stronger than the original plate, so it can be used to run off many more copies.

This new industrial process was a key factor in the rise of print media. Also, the machines made a noise that the French called *cliché*. To print with a stereotype press was *clicher* – literally, to make clichés.

Stereotypes and clichés, in our modern usage, reflect these origins. Both phenomena are the product of repetition. A saying becomes a cliché when it is overused. A stereotype is an image, or a description, that we have seen many, many times before and which we take as truth.

In the two hundred years or so since stereotype printing was invented, people have largely taken over the process of reproducing hackneyed images from the mainstream media. Each of us is a mouthpiece, and a thought space, for simple, stylised ideas about other people.

Table 3.1: Commonly held gender stereotypes.

Positive female	Negative male
Warm	Cold
Nurturing	Harsh
Caring	Rude
Kind	Selfish
Loving	Aloof
Forgiving	Hostile
Negative female	**Positive male**
Weak	Power
Timid	Strong
Yielding	Leader
Surrendering	Confident
Fragile	Dominant
Follower	Bold

(adapted from Rudman, Greenwald and McGhee, 2001[11])

Stereotypes in general form the foundation of all our learning, since they encourage us to respond to certain distinctions and honour certain categories.

This is the basic organisational equipment we need to negotiate the world, and you could say that all subsequent education is a matter of learning new categorisation schemas and how to stock them. Our feelings of "rightness" when we categorise correctly may originate in this early conditioning. Adults are still comforted by the fact that trains go "choo choo", even though they don't.

From a very young age, we learn ideologies surrounding the roles of men and women in society. Stereotypes – the handy pack of mental associations about men and women – are embedded in these ideologies.

For example, from birth the kind of clothing given to girls and boys is different. In our contemporary culture, pink is for girls and blue is for boys. These are socially constructed traditions that help us categorise and identity the gender of babies.

Research shows that children as young as two years of age know about gender stereotypes.[12-14] Using a method known as the preferential looking procedure, which measures toddlers' preference for different stimuli, Hill and Flom (2007)[12] found that toddlers spent longer looking at a person performing an activity that was contrary to their gender stereotype – for example, a man putting on lipstick or a woman shaving. The longer periods of time spent looking at activities which run counter to gender stereotypes suggests puzzlement or surprise on the part of the child. No differences in duration of gaze were noted when gender-neutral activities were performed. It seems we are learning activities and traits associated with each gender from a very young age.

Since embarking on this book, the authors have been paying close attention to the things we hear adults say to children and, indeed, what we say to our own child. Here's some of what we heard:

> Said to a little girl when she suggested climbing a tree: "You can't climb that tree… I'm sure you are a boy in disguise."
> To a little girl playing with a yellow toy mechanical digger: "Girls play with pink toys."
> About a boisterous and rather ill-behaved child: "He's such a boy."

> A mother about her son who is very curious: "He's into everything."
> The same mother about her daughter who is very curious: "She's such a girl."

These small remarks act as constant reinforcement of the roles and behaviours associated with each gender. Not surprisingly, they are quickly assimilated into a child's beliefs about the way the world is structured. We have also been listening to what children say to adults:

> "Girls are fairies and boys are elves."
> "Girls like pink and boys like blue."

Even as adults the same process can occur. For example, do you pay more attention when the pilot of your aircraft is female? Or a nurse on the ward is male? Without realising it, we have expectations about the gender of a role and we become aware of these expectations when they are not met or are confounded. It is nothing to be ashamed of, but it is something that we need to acknowledge if we are going to do something about it.

Notice that this doesn't mean babies are born with innate ideas about what activities are proper to males and females. Young children are being *taught* gender stereotypes.

Research shows that gender stereotypes are both consistent across cultures and time[15] and are stable.[16] Therefore, stereotypes develop based on experience and lead to the mental associations we hold about a target object. They are activated when we are exposed to that target.[17] Often described as mental shortcuts, they enable us to rapidly process and make sense of a vast amount of information in order to form an impression of someone. Since stereotypes are based on beliefs and not facts, they are often faulty and lead to false assumptions, judgements and decision-making. This phenomenon is referred to as bias.

To illustrate this, we split a large number of senior executives in a financial services firm into two groups. Each group was given a photograph of the same woman and a list of questions about her: her name, profession, hobbies, marital status, and so on. One group identified her as Charlotte, a married woman who worked as a scientist. The other group thought she was Chardonnay, a single mother living off benefits.

Although the photos were of the same person, context and dress were altered. With these changes, a very different portrait emerged in the minds of the viewers. When someone is disadvantaged as a result of the faulty concepts and stereotypes that have been applied to them, the biased outcome is discrimination.

Fig 3.1: The Impact of Context.

Stereotypes can operate both explicitly and implicitly. When they operate explicitly, we know they are playing a role in our behaviour, and we may or may not take steps to control their impact. When stereotypes are operating implicitly, they are working automatically and shaping our behaviour without us being consciously aware of their influence.

But are stereotypes truths?

We can start the process of challenging the supposed gender divide by questioning the surface properties of objects and settings that are supposedly distinguished by gender.

Take the popular toy kitchen sold in Britain by the Early Learning Centre. This is a child-sized cooker/sink combo with pans, spoons and other plastic accessories (which you will find later in unexpected places around the house). The item comes in two forms: red and blue or cream and pink. Which one do you buy for a little boy?

The toy kitchen functions in exactly the same way whichever colour scheme you buy. The play value is in putting things inside other things, assembling sequences of actions and asking Mum and Dad what they would like for dinner. There's nothing remotely specific to male or female traits or roles in any of these activities. But the surface attributes of the product lead us to believe that one is more suitable for boys and the other is more suitable for girls.

In the same way, surface attributes of men and women lead us to believe they are different in the way they function. For example, men rarely wear high heels. This suggests men are more practically minded – they may need to evade a tiger on the way to the station. Men typically wear a more restricted set of colours and styles than women, which suggests that, in humans, females have the sexual display function. (Although in the 2013 heatwave, Swedish train drivers did opt to wear skirts to work as a way to overcome the shorts ban imposed by the operator.)

Dress may seem trivial, but it is a powerful means of signalling. Explicit and implicit dress codes rule our lives and they appear to encode universal and eternal truths about the two sexes. Yet a little historical research suggests the relationship between dress and gender is complex and mutable. The costume dramas we enjoy on TV bring this variability vividly to life. When men were wearing tights and wigs, which sex was sexually displaying? What about the Elizabethan codpiece?

Dress is such a powerful means of communicating about gender that it is often at the forefront of attempts to change gendered thinking. The right to wear trousers is a clear example of asserted equality between the sexes, since being restricted to wearing skirts bars women from many activities. Clothing is a stereotype enhancer because it accentuates the physical differences between men and women. We see the difference and we also believe that there are other differences beneath the surface. Clothing can also delineate the roles that we expect the gender to play: it wasn't that long ago when women police officers in the Britain not only had to wear skirts but were also routinely issued with a handbag. It is no surprise, therefore, to find that women officers were excluded from dealing with certain types of crime, such as rioting. The abrupt transition between the Edwardian "hourglass" and the flapper "cylinder" speaks volumes about women's self-assertion after the First World War.

So gender stereotypes are learned – there is ample evidence that there are no true differences between the sexes. Our beliefs about differences originate from our ideologies about the roles men and women should hold. We now turn to the stronghold stereotypes have on our belief system, and the consequences of leaving them unchallenged.

Stereotypes influence expectations

Stereotypes influence what we pay attention to, how we interpret that information and what we remember. Even if we overcome one of these elements, the next one is there as a hurdle to ensure our beliefs remain intact.

First, attention. As noted in the preface, people are "cognitive misers"[18] – we want to process information in a way that requires minimal effort. We are therefore motivated to see things in a way that is consistent with our well-established belief systems. Stereotypes direct our attention towards information that confirms our beliefs. We have a natural tendency to seek and acknowledge confirmatory information, thereby strengthening the very stereotypes that are controlling our attention. Our attention is directed towards consistent information and away from inconsistent information.[19] As a result, stereotypes and the expectations they create often go unchallenged.

Next, interpretation. Even when we pay attention to inconsistent information, we have a tendency to interpret the information in a way that is consistent with our expectations. The same behaviour performed by a man and a woman may be interpreted very differently.[20] Behaviour may be described as "laid-back" when observed in a man but "timid" when observed in a woman.[21] Stereotypes also influence interpretations of performance and the attribution of success. When a woman succeeds, particularly in what is believed to be a "male" task, her success is attributed to effort, luck, or ease of the task, rather than skill.[22] When a man succeeds, his success is often attributed to internal factors such as ability and skill. Furthermore, when a man fails on a "male" task, his failure is attributed to lack of effort[23] or bad luck, whereas a woman's failure is attributed to low ability. Women are not allowed to have a skill even when they demonstrate one, while men are granted a skill even when they fail to demonstrate it. Our interpretations of events are therefore being constantly twisted to fit the framework of our expectations.

Finally, we have the element of memory. Expectations weigh heavily on what we remember. We are more likely to remember information which is consistent with our expectations than information which is inconsistent. Worse than this, our memory can lead us to make up the existence of expectation-consistent information even when there is no such real evidence.[24] So when a woman behaves in a stereotypically consistent way, by for example being caring, this is more likely to be remembered than if she behaves contrary to expectations – for example, by being assertive and showing leadership qualities. And it gets worse: we misremember certain behaviours when they run counter to our expectations. Basically, we have a tendency to make things up in order to preserve our beliefs.

Surprisingly – or perhaps not – the news that girls are innately better than boys at physics hasn't filtered through to the popular press. Why not? Not because it's not true, but because it doesn't jibe with what we expect to hear. This is one small, objectively measured, evidenced difference that no one is interested in exaggerating.

Received wisdom deceives. We all know, don't we, how much more women chatter than men and books on gender differences typically point this out. Australian scientist Karl Kruszelnicki[25] noticed two interesting pairs of numbers. Each pair purports to measure the difference in the amount of talking that women and men do. One is 20,000 words per day versus 7,000. The other is 30,000 versus 12,000. One set of numbers comes from a book called *The Female Brain*, the other from the Ladies Golf Journey website – though it doesn't really matter which pair comes from which source, since both are wrong.

It would be illuminating to find out the right ratio. Except there is no such thing. There will never be a correct measurement, because women do not talk more than men. It's our expectation that leads us to think that they do. Research by Culter and Scott in 1990[26] clearly demonstrates this. When showing people videos of men and women in conversation, even though the amount they spoke was equal, both male and female listeners rated the women as contributing to the conversation more than men; that is, they believed women spoke the most.

Kruszelnicki points out that an exhaustive literature review carried out as long ago as 1993 concluded there is no difference in the amount men and women talk. Further studies carried out since then have found no significant difference between men and women – the largest variations in talkativeness being *within* genders rather than across them. So our popular, long held, notions about the relative talkativeness of the genders turns out to be nothing more than empty talk. It is the expectation created by stereotypes that leads to the belief that women talk more than men.

Descriptive stereotypes and their impact at work

As mentioned previously, stereotypes have two forms: descriptive and prescriptive. We will consider prescriptive stereotypes in more detail in the next chapter, but take a closer look at descriptive stereotypes here.

Descriptive stereotypes are beliefs about how men and women differ. They can be thought of as faulty programming in our brains, stemming from the ideologies we have been exposed to. Their application is due to faulty belief systems, which are often automatic, and so their impact is unintentional. Despite being unintentional, these faulty belief systems have a major negative impact on women in work. Descriptive stereotypes trigger questions over a woman's competence to perform certain roles, which will hinder a woman's progression.

Compliments and innuendo

With other types of bias such as those associated with, for example, ethnicity, disability or age, negative terms are more often used to describe the outgroup. But a strange thing has occurred over the last twenty to thirty years: the use of negative stereotypes to describe women, but not men, has become increasingly unacceptable. This would be a good thing but for the corresponding rise in the use of positive stereotypes. The ideology that women and men are different and complementary is firmly embedded, with an apparently "balanced" use of positive stereotypes unique to gender. For example, men are decisive but women are warm. This construction sounds like an affirmative to gender differences, but it is more akin to changing the subject.

The affirmative language associated with gender stereotypes means their use can be seen as a compliment. Furthermore, stereotypical descriptions of women are often more flattering than those used to describe men. Women are warm, caring and understanding, whereas men are focused, competitive and aggressive. For example, Nigel Nicholson's[27] descriptions of women are all positive, but socially oriented, whereas his descriptions of men are more negative but more closely associated with leadership.

Additionally, the positive but different qualities attached to men and women are seen to complement each other. You often hear men and women being described like this in organisations: women bring something different to the organisation because they are softer, better at relationships, more empathetic and men are strategic, visionary and task-focused. It's so yin and yang... Or is it just an updated version of the patronising male view of his partner as his "better half"?

If gender stereotypes are made up of positive attributes, then what's the problem? It would appear that the stereotypes we hold support the valuing of difference. But although the traits associated with women are positive in the abstract, they are not those that are valued or deemed necessary in a business context – and especially not in a leadership role. Many of the traits stereotypically associated with women are not those stereotypically associated with leadership or male gender type roles. How many leaders do you hear described primarily as warm and caring? As such, while on the surface positive stereotypes attached to women appear to be compliments, they can and do hinder women's career progression.

Studying over 600 letters of recommendation for academic positions over an eight-year period, researchers[28] found that letters of recommendation were written differently for men and women. The letters for women were described with stereotypical feminine qualities (communal, i.e. more socially oriented and people-focused) whereas those for men were described with stereotypical masculine qualities (agentic, i.e. getting things done and task-focused). Furthermore, communal traits were inversely related to hiring decisions regardless of gender. If your organisation relies on internal references in its evaluation and promotion processes then this may be an interesting area to look at. The way we describe men and women needs to change – we are lazy and often rely on stereotypes.

The positive and often complimentary nature of male and female stereotypes helps to increase the perception that inequality is fair, legitimate and justifiable.[29] In fact, the whole concept of valuing individual difference perpetuates the myth that there are differences between men and women which impact on performance at work. This serves as a way to maintain the status quo by giving justifiable reasons why men and women should be in different roles and positions based on their unique traits.

Members of subordinated groups, however, are often complicit in their subordination.[29] For a woman, being described in positive terms is easier to assimilate into her self-identity than being described in negative terms. We prefer to describe ourselves in positive terms.[30] You rarely hear a woman walking around saying she is not strategic or decisive.

Let's be clear: positive stereotypes are as damaging as negative ones because they are still stereotypes. They are inaccurate representations of the true abilities of men and women but, because they are expressed affirmatively, people (men *and* women) are less likely to challenge them and consequently are more prepared to use them in decision-making. Don't be fooled: the use of positive stereotypes for women is one of the ways in which their progress is being hindered. The subtle damage done by these deceptively attractive stereotypes is widely neglected, and further evidence comes from a phenomenon known as the innuendo effect.[31]

Of relevance here is work done by Susan Fiske and colleagues[32] that has shown we classify stereotyped groups across two dimensions – competence and warmth. According to the stereotype content model, while ingroups are often viewed on these universal dimensions as both warm and competent, outgroups are often perceived as being positive on one dimension but negative on the other. For example, housewives are often perceived as warm but not competent, whereas professional women are often seen as competent but not warm.

When receiving positive information about another person and where relevant information is left out, negative inferences will be drawn on the omitted dimension (warmth or competence), resulting in lower evaluations of the individual.[31] Since women are often described as empathetic, good listeners and team players and men as decisive, logical and task-focused, we will draw the conclusion that women do not possess the other qualities; that is, that they are *not* decisive, logical or task-focused.

So, describing a woman as warm but omitting anything about her competence will lead to negative inferences about her competence. Although the same is true for men, the damage to them is less severe. Describing men as competent but omitting anything about their warmth will do less harm, since it is competence that is valued when it comes to progression in organisations.

Omissions are important. In the modern workplace it is less and less acceptable to express prejudices overtly. So in order to preserve their self-image, a person who is biased against another is more likely to omit information than openly express their concern. However, our brains don't miss the unspoken. We process implicit information alongside explicit information. If one dimension is omitted from a description, then we assume the individual lacks that dimension – and the competences that go along with it.[31] It's as if the accumulation of positive ascriptions serves to underline the "missing" attributes.

Since an unmentioned dimension has a powerful effect on our judgement, it is important that we include both dimensions in every evaluative description we make of an individual. If we don't, an unspoken "but..." will undermine the rationality of the decision-making process, allowing bias to distort our actions.

Lack of fit: how expectations impact on performance ratings and promotion

Stereotypes lead to expectations about how a man and woman will perform in certain roles. When a woman is being considered for a role in an area traditionally seen as male, say a leadership position, the stereotypical traits she is thought to possess (empathy, kindness and so on) are compared to the stereotypical traits associated with leadership (such as assertiveness and decisiveness). Because the leadership prototype is constructed on stereotypically male traits,[33] when a woman is matched against the prototype the expectation is that she will fall short, whereas a man will be evaluated favourably. This "lack of fit"[34] results in women being more negatively evaluated than men. The woman is not seen as having the competence to perform the role and thus fares worse than her male counterparts when pay, performance evaluation and promotion are considered.[21]

Performance ratings are influenced by a range of factors:

- The nature of the task: women were more negatively evaluated when they were involved in stereotypically masculine tasks as opposed to stereotypically feminine tasks.[35]

- The roles men and women are in: when women were in line manager roles as opposed to staff roles, they received lower performance ratings compared to both their male counterparts in the same positions and women in staff roles.[36]

- The number of women already working in a stereotypically male area: women's competence and performance were rated significantly lower than men's in parts of the organisation where women were under-represented, but not in parts where they were not.[37]

At the same time, women are penalised for being in non-stereotypical roles and rewarded for being in the typecast ones.

We would like to believe that performance ratings are related to promotion decisions, so that the best performers are the ones in line to be promoted. This is supposed to be the purpose of the system, after all. In fact, performance ratings have been found to be more strongly related to promotion for women than they are for men. Those women who had been promoted had received higher performance ratings for the two years prior to elevation than their male counterparts, after controlling for age, tenure, education and organisational level.[36] In other words, women had to be *outperforming* men in order to be promoted.

Making people accountable for hiring decisions is generally a good thing, as long as the policy is evaluated properly. In these situations, women are more likely than men to get on to a shortlist for a job, but less likely than men to be hired for the same job.[38] This may be one reason why we often see healthy talent pipelines with equal proportions of men and women on "the list", but little conversion when it comes to promotion. More evidence of competence is needed to overcome the negative performance expectation associated with women in male gender typed roles. In psychological jargon, the stereotypes prompt lower minimal standards for entry for women but higher confirmatory standards that they can do the job.[39]

Ambiguity of task success

Stereotypes also influence who we regard as having made a significant contribution to a piece of work, particularly if it is unclear who was responsible for the task success. When there is ambiguity over who was responsible for the success of a task, we are more likely to attribute the success to a man than a woman. In such situations women are rated as less competent, less influential and less likely to have played a leadership role than men.[40] Negative expectations of woman's ability to perform in a man's role lead us to question whether she contributed to the success. For example, in one law firm we worked in, a senior male lawyer was promoted to partner because of the new clients he had brought in. A female senior lawyer was denied partnership despite bringing in more new business from her existing clients, this achievement being evaluated as less worthy since she had not originally won the work.

This point is important, since nowadays much of the work we do is structured in teams. In addition, there has been a marked rise in virtual team-working over recent years. Such ways of working have greater potential to mask individual contribution and so create ambiguity over who was responsible for success. This can be very damaging to women, given that we are likely to attribute the success to men.

To overcome this tendency, we need to:

- Provide information on each individual's unique contribution

- Verify that a woman played a role in the success

- Provide clear evidence that the woman has succeeded previously in male typed roles.[40]

Stereotype threat

When descriptive stereotypes are salient, there is a risk that they will impact on performance. Referred to in the literature as stereotype threat,[41] this phenomenon occurs when someone lives up – or, more accurately, down – to the expectations placed on them. It has been demonstrated time and time again in the research.

Take the example of driving a car. We all know women are useless at driving, don't we? Well, that all depends on the salient expectation present. When women were told that men are better drivers, they were more than twice as likely to collide with jaywalking pedestrians in a simulated task.[42]

Stereotype threat has been shown to play a role in a number of domains. Reminding women of the stereotype that they are not good at maths diminished their performance in maths tasks[43,44] and their ability to learn maths rules.[45] One notable area where stereotype threat has an impact is in the boardroom, where the stereotype that women are less effective is prevalent. Nielson and Huse (2010)[46] found that when women were perceived as unequal board members their contribution to board decision-making was reduced. Furthermore, when a woman encounters a stereotype threat, she may prefer to avoid leadership roles altogether.[47]

So, if someone is confronted with a negative stereotype about themselves, such as being labelled as not being competent at a task, there is a high risk they will fulfil the prophecy. This phenomenon is thought to result from the individual monitoring their own performance more closely so as to avoid failure,[48,49] leading to an increase in cognitive load. Working memory capacity comes under greater pressure, reducing performance in a wide variety of cognitive, social and sensorimotor tasks (for an overview see Schmader, Johns and Forbes[50]). So the next time a man is in the passenger seat tut-tutting away at the woman's driving, it may be worth informing him that it is actually his behaviour that is likely to provoke an accident!

Research has found that women's performance in spatial tasks increases significantly when negative stereotypes are countered with positive messages.[51] Furthermore, getting people to affirm their most important value can reduce the impacts of stereotype threat,[52] as can simply informing people that the stereotype is inaccurate.[53]

In the same way that negative stereotypes can impair performance, positive stereotypes can enhance performance.[44] When men and women were primed with gender stereotypes about negotiation – men are often believed to be better than women at this – it led to men's performance being enhanced.[54] Another area where strong gender stereotypes are held is in mathematics – women are supposedly worse than men at solving difficult maths problems.[55] Research by Spencer, Steele and Quinn[44] found that men only outperformed women in solving difficult maths problems when they were told that gender differences had been found in this domain – that is, men had been found to be better. Furthermore, those men who had been told of the gender differences also outperformed men who had *not* been told about gender differences. Our expectations can increase performance as well as inhibit it.

Things just get worse when a woman becomes a mother

As noted previously, when meeting people we assess them on two universal dimensions – competence and warmth. Research has explored what happens to ratings of men and women on these dimensions when they hold two roles simultaneously, for example those of professional and parent.

When a professional woman becomes a mother she gains the perception from others of being warm but is no longer perceived as competent. However, when a man becomes a parent he gains warmth while retaining the perception of being competent.[56] Parenthood, in an organisational context, diminishes a woman but enlarges a man.

This effect is particularly damaging for women since, when it comes to assessing people for recruitment, promotion and training opportunities, it is competence that matters above all else.[56] This is particularly true when it comes to high-status jobs and leadership positions. Here, warmth becomes irrelevant and the leadership prototype rules. Studies[56] have demonstrated that participants were less interested in rewarding working mothers. While men benefit from the dual identity of parenthood, women are penalised.

We habitually see impending parenthood as a sign that a woman is about to retreat from, or be expelled from, the world of work. For example, when a woman is pregnant, she is perceived as being less competent and less qualified for promotion when compared to a non-pregnant woman, even though both women are observed performing the exact same task.[57]

So, once a woman becomes pregnant or is known to have children the perception of her competence changes. She is seen as having fewer of the traits required to be successful in the workplace, and more of the traits associated with being successful as a homemaker. However, although we typically make this error, we don't necessarily *like* making it. It's not a judgement we can comfortably defend. This means that if there is another factor available to justify why we discriminated against the person, we will use it. For example, a woman was less likely to be hired, promoted or trained because she telecommuted for part of the week, not because she had recently become a mother. But participants did not apply the same penalties to men who telecommuted, which can only mean they were using telecommuting as a justifiable excuse.[56]

To sum up, there was a time when negative stereotypes were expressed freely, but this rarely happens in public these days. However, positive stereotypes are regularly endorsed publicly because they are seen as expressing something good about people. Therefore, while people may not endorse negative stereotypes, they will happily endorse positive stereotypes. They are less likely to see positive stereotypes as inappropriate to a decision-making process, meaning they won't correct for their influence. As a consequence, decision-making is likely to be infused with inaccurate information.

There is mounting evidence that different standards of performance are set for men and women. When it comes to promotion, women are held to stricter performance standards. When working with organisations, women often tell us they believe they need to work harder than their male counterparts in order to succeed. It is clear that such perceptions are supported by the research. Swedish researchers found, for example, that female academics had to be 250% more productive than men to obtain the same ratings of competence as men.

Women need to prove themselves more and provide more evidence of their competence. Men, on the other hand, enjoy the invisible support of "the benefit of the doubt", which is known as the "majority advantage". This leads to men gaining opportunities such as mentoring, contacts and trust simply because they are men. Research like this casts serious doubt on organisations which claim to operate a meritocracy. Different standards can be used without recognising that this is happening, undermining the very meaning of merit.

In short, we are predisposed to view a woman negatively when assessing her against traits required for male sex typed roles. We *expect* women not to perform as well as men when the task or role is male sex typed. This leads to us evaluating women more negatively than men in such situations.

Descriptive gender stereotypes are faulty associations in the brain. As such, we are not consciously aware of them and their influence on our judgements and decision-making. They can best be combated by raising our awareness of them. By bringing unconscious stereotypes to conscious attention, we can question their validity.

References

1. Blasi G. 'Advocacy against the stereotype: Lessons from cognitive social psychology.' *UCLA Law Review* 2001; 1241–1282.

2. Eagly AH. *Sex Differences in Social Behavior.* Psychology Press; 1987.

3. Glick P, Fiske ST. 'Sexism and other " isms": Independence, status, and the ambivalent content of stereotypes.' In Swann WB Jr, Langlois JH and Gilbert LA (eds), *Sexism and Stereotypes in Modern Society: The Gender Science of Janet Taylor Spence.* American Psychological Association; 1999, pp. 193–221. doi: 10.1037/10277-008.

4. Banaji MR, Greenwald AG. 'Implicit gender stereotyping in judgments of fame.' *Journal of Personality and Social Psychology* 1995; 68(2): 181.

5. Banaji MR, Hardin CD. 'Automatic stereotyping.' *Psychological Science* 1996; 7(3): 136 –141.

6. Banaji MR, Hardin C, Rothman AJ. 'Implicit stereotyping in person judgment.' *Journal of Personality and Social Psychology* 1993; 65(2): 272.

7. Blair IV, Banaji MR. 'Automatic and controlled processes in stereotype priming.' *Journal of Personality and Social Psychology* 1996; 70(6): 1142.

8. Gerdes EP, Kelman JH. 'Sex discrimination: Effects of sex-role incongruence, evaluator sex, and stereotypes.' *Basic and Applied Social Psychology* 1981; 2(3): 219–226. doi:10.1207/s15324834basp0203_5.

9. Glick P. 'Trait-based and sex-based discrimination in occupational prestige, occupational salary, and hiring.' *Sex Roles* 1991; 25(5-6): 351–378.

10. Pratto F, Stallworth LM, Sidanius J, Siers B. 'The gender gap in occupational role attainment: a social dominance approach.' *Journal of Personality and Social Psychology* 1997; 72(1): 37.

11. Rudman LA, Greenwald AG, McGhee DE. 'Implicit self-concept and evaluative implicit gender stereotypes: Self and ingroup share desirable traits.' *Personality and Social Psychology Bulletin* 2001; 27(9): 1164–1178. doi:10.1177/0146167201279009.

12. Hill SE, Flom R. '18- and 24-month-olds' discrimination of gender-consistent and inconsistent activities.' *Infant Behavior and Development* 2007; 30(1): 168–173. doi:10.1016/j.infbeh.2006.08.003.

13. Serbin LA, Poulin-Dubois D, Eichstedt JA. 'Infants' responses to gender-inconsistent events.' *Infancy* 2002; 3(4): 531–542. doi:10.1207/S15327078IN0304_07.

14. Poulin-Dubois D, Serbin LA, Derbyshire A. 'Toddlers' intermodal and verbal knowledge about gender.' *Merrill-Palmer Quarterly (1982-)* 1998; 44(3): 338–354.

15. Williams JE, Best DL. *Measuring Sex Stereotypes.* Sage Publications; 1990.

16. Lueptow LB, Garovich L, Lueptow MB. 'The persistence of gender stereotypes in the face of changing sex roles: Evidence contrary to the sociocultural model.' *Ethology and Sociobiology* 1995; 16(6): 509–530.

17. Devine PG. 'Stereotypes and prejudice: Their automatic and controlled components.' *Journal of Personality and Social Psychology* 1989; 56(1): 5.

18. Fiske, ST, Taylor, SE. *Social Cognition*. Addison-Wesley; 1984.

19. Johnson JT, Judd CM. 'Overlooking the incongruent: Categorization biases in the identification of political statements.' *Journal of Personality and Social Psychology* 1983; 45(5): 978.

20. Kunda Z, Sinclair L, Griffin D. 'Equal ratings but separate meanings: Stereotypes and the construal of traits.' *Journal of Personality and Social Psychology* 1997; 72(4): 720–734. doi:10.1037/0022-3514.72.4.720.

21. Heilman ME, Parks-Stamm EJ. 'Gender stereotypes in the workplace: Obstacles to women's career progress.' *Advances in Group Processes* 2007; 24: 47–77. doi:10.1016/S0882-6145(07)24003-2.3d.

22. Igen DR, Youtz MA. 'Factors affecting the evaluation, and development of minorities in organizations.' In Rowland KM and Ferris GR (eds), *Research in Personnel and Human Resources Management: A Research Annual* (4, 307–337). JAI; 1986.

23. Swim JK, Sanna LJ. 'He's skilled, she's lucky: A meta-analysis of observers' attributions for women's and men's successes and failures.' *Personality and Social Psychology Bulletin* 1996; 22(5): 507–519.

24. Fiske ST, Neuberg SL. 'A continuum of impression formation, from category-based to individuating processes: Influences of information and motivation on attention and interpretation.' In: MP Zanna (ed.), *Advances in Experimental Social Psychology*. Academic Press; 1990, pp. 1–74.

25. At: http://www.abc.net.au/science/articles/2010/03/31/2861505.htm. Accessed 20 September 2013.

26. Cutler A, Scott DR. 'Speaker sex and perceived apportionment of talk.' *Applied Psycholinguistics* 1990; 11(3): 253–272.

27. Nicholson N. *Managing the Human Animal*. Texere Publishing; 2000.

28. Madera JM, Hebl MR, Martin RC. 'Gender and letters of recommendation for academia: Agentic and communal differences.' *Journal of Applied Psychology* 2009; 94(6): 1591–1599. doi:10.1037/a0016539.

29. Jost JT, Kay AC. 'Exposure to benevolent sexism and complementary gender stereotypes: Consequences for specific and diffuse forms of system justification.' *Journal of Personality and Social Psychology* 2005; 88(3): 498–509. doi:10.1037/0022-3514.88.3.498.

30. Greenwald AG, Banaji MR, Rudman LA, Farnham SD, Nosek BA, Mellott DS. 'A unified theory of implicit attitudes, stereotypes, self-esteem, and self-concept.' *Psychological Review* 2002; 109(1): 3–25.

31. Kervyn N, Bergsieker HB, Fiske ST. 'The innuendo effect: Hearing the positive but inferring the negative.' *Journal of Experimental Social Psychology* 2012; 48(1): 77–85. doi:10.1016/j.jesp.2011.08.001.

32. Fiske ST, Cuddy AJC, Glick P, Xu J. 'A model of (often mixed) stereotype content: Competence and warmth respectively follow from perceived status and competition.' *Journal of Personality and Social Psychology* 2002; 82(6): 878–902.doi:10.1037//0022-3514.82.6.878.

33. Offermann LR, Kennedy JK, Wirtz PW. 'Implicit leadership theories: Content, structure, and

generalizability.' *The Leadership Quarterly* 1994; 5(1): 43–58.

34. Heilman ME. 'Sex bias in work settings: The lack of fit model.' *Research in Organizational Behavior* 1983; 5: 269–298.

35. Swim J, Borgida E, Maruyama G, Myers DG. 'Joan McKay versus John McKay: Do gender stereotypes bias evaluations?' *Psychological Bulletin* 1989; 105(3): 409.

36. Lyness KS, Heilman ME. 'When fit is fundamental: Performance evaluations and promotions of upper-level female and male managers.' *Journal of Applied Psychology* 2006; 91(4): 777–785. doi:10.1037/0021-9010.91.4.777.

37. Pazy A, Oron I. 'Sex proportion and performance evaluation among high-ranking military officers.' *Journal of Organizational Behavior* 2001; 22(6): 689–702. doi:10.1002/job.109.

38. Biernat M, Fuegen K. 'Shifting standards and the evaluation of competence: Complexity in gender-based judgment and decision making.' *Journal of Social Issues* 2002; 57(4): 707–724.

39. Biernat MM, Kobrynowicz DD. 'Gender- and race-based standards of competence: Lower minimum standards but higher ability standards for devalued groups.' *Journal of Personality and Social Psychology* 1997; 72(3): 544–557. doi:10.1037/0022-3514.72.3.544.

40. Heilman ME, Haynes MC. 'No credit where credit is due: Attributional rationalization of women's success in male–female teams.' *Journal of Applied Psychology* 2005; 90(5): 905–916. doi:10.1037/0021-9010.90.5.905.

41. Steele CMC, Aronson JJ. 'Stereotype threat and the intellectual test performance of African Americans.' *Journal of Personality and Social Psychology* 1995; 69(5): 797–811. doi:10.1037/0022-3514.69.5.797.

42. Yeung NCJN, Hippel von CC. 'Stereotype threat increases the likelihood that female drivers in a simulator run over jaywalkers.' *Accident Analysis and Prevention* 2008; 40(2): 8. doi:10.1016/j.aap.2007.09.003.

43. Krendl AC, Richeson JA, Kelley WM, Heatherton TF. 'The negative consequences of threat: A functional magnetic resonance imaging investigation of the neural mechanisms underlying women's underperformance in math.' *Psychological Science* 2008; 19(2): 168–175.

44. Spencer SJ, Steele CM, Quinn DM. 'Stereotype threat and women's math performance.' *Journal of Experimental Social Psychology* 1999; 35(1): 4–28.

45. Rydell RJ, Rydell MT, Boucher KL. 'The effect of negative performance stereotypes on learning.' *Journal of Personality and Social Psychology* 2010; 99(6): 883–896. doi:10.1037/a0021139.

46. Nielsen S, Huse M. 'Women directors' contribution to board decision-making and strategic involvement: The role of equality perception.' *European Management Review* 2010; 7(1): 16–29.

47. Davies PG, Spencer SJ, Steele CM. 'Clearing the air: Identity safety moderates the effects of stereotype threat on women's leadership aspirations.' *Journal of Personality and Social Psychology* 2005; 88(2): 276–287. doi:10.1037/0022-3514.88.2.276.

48. Forbes CE, Schmader T, Allen JJB. 'The role of devaluing and discounting in performance monitoring: A neurophysiological study of minorities under threat.' *Social Cognitive and Affective Neuroscience* 2008; 3(3): 253–261. doi:10.1093/scan/nsn012.

49. Seibt B, Förster J. 'Stereotype threat and performance: How self-stereotypes influence processing by inducing regulatory foci.' *Journal of Personality and Social Psychology* 2004; 87(1): 38–56. doi:10.1037/0022-3514.87.1.38.

50. Schmader T, Johns M, Forbes C. 'An integrated process model of stereotype threat effects on performance.' *Psychological Review* 2008; 115(2): 336–356. doi:10.1037/0033-295X.115.2.336.

51. Estes Z, Felker S. 'Confidence mediates the sex difference in mental rotation performance.' *Archives of Sexual Behavior* 2011; 41(3): 557–570. doi:10.1007/s10508-011-9875-5.

52. Inzlicht M, Kang SK. 'Stereotype threat spillover: How coping with threats to social identity affects aggression, eating, decision making, and attention.' *Journal of Personality and Social Psychology* 2010; 99(3): 467–481. doi:10.1037/a0018951.

53. Johns M, Schmader T, Martens A. 'Knowing is half the battle: Teaching stereotype threat as a means of improving women's math performance.' *Psychological Science* 2005; 16 (3): 175–179.

54. Thompson LJKL, Galinsky 'A. battle of the sexes: gender stereotype confirmation and reactance in negotiations.' *Journal of Personality and Social Psychology* 2001; 80(6): 942–958.

55. Benbow CPC, Stanley JCJ. 'Sex differences in mathematical ability: Fact or artifact?' *Science* 1980; 210(4475): 1262–1264.

56. Cuddy AJC, Fiske ST, Glick P. 'When professionals become mothers, warmth doesn't cut the ice.' *Journal of Social Issues* 2004; 60(4): 701–718.

57. Halpert JA, Wilson ML, Hickman JL. 'Pregnancy as a source of bias in performance appraisals.' *Journal of Organizational Behavior* 2006; 14(7): 649–663.

4

THOU SHALT (NOT): THE IMPACT OF PRESCRIPTIVE STEREOTYPES

In Chapter 3 we considered descriptive stereotypes – beliefs about how men and women are different. In this chapter we turn to look at prescriptive stereotypes and the potency they have in the workplace.

Prescriptive stereotypes are concerned with beliefs about what men and women should be like, how they should behave and the traits we should see them exhibit. For example, it's well known that "a woman's work is never done". The virtuous woman "also rises while it is yet night, and provides food for her household" (Proverbs 31:15). (Incidentally, *The Skeptics' Annotated Bible* lists 39 "insults to women" in the book of Leviticus.[1])

These maxims sound simply descriptive – messages about how the world is. But while they are couched as statements of the obvious, they are really assertions. The Bible does not bother to say "grass is green". If any scripture-based religion were to mention grass, it might be to say "grass is mown" or "grass is not to be walked on". Proverbs are a matter of indoctrination, not observation.

Combating prescriptive stereotypes requires different interventions from the descriptive type. Prescriptive stereotypes are more likely to be consciously held and motivationally driven, so merely raising awareness of their existence is unlikely to prove effective.

Where do prescriptive stereotypes come from?

Every dominant group depends on subordinate groups.[2] Since it is to the dominant group's advantage to uphold these prestige differences and dependencies, they will be motivated to do so. This is where prescriptive stereotypes come in: they serve to maintain the status quo. Slave owners see slaves as inferior human beings whose role is to carry out menial and physically demanding tasks. In turn the slaves see their role as tending to the needs of their masters. To be winners there have to be losers – it is a zero sum game. For this relationship to remain in place both parties have to accept not only their own status but that of the other.

This is especially true of gender. Generally speaking, it is to men's advantage that a woman's role is defined as being in the home and caring for the family, thus leaving them to take on the role of breadwinner and provider. This also means that the higher status and better remunerated positions in society will be taken by men. The prescriptive stereotypes, determining the role of each gender, serve to maintain the world as we know it. Both parties are dependent on one another to carry out their allotted roles because without that tacit agreement society, as we constructed it, is irrevocably changed.

Maintaining the status quo requires a system of rewards and punishments, both explicit and implicit. One strategy is to highlight the differences between the groups in order to bolster the case that each should stick to areas where their abilities are best suited – either the workplace or the home, leading or supporting. Glick and Fiske[2] say that dependence between the groups is vital, and when there is a decrease in dependence there is also a reduction in prescribed ways of behaving. For example, the prescriptive stereotypes associated with white Americans and African Americans have declined because there is now less dependence between the groups.

Enforcing ways to behave and penalising people when they break these norms helps maintain the status differences between the groups. Now, some may agree with this description but say that it applies to previous generations but not our own. But we need to accept that this system is still active. Denying its persistence only delays any attempts to remedy the situation.

The "Shoulds" and "Should Nots" of gendered behaviour

Although the content of prescriptive and descriptive stereotypes is the same, their application leads to different consequences. As noted in Chapter 3, descriptive stereotypes raise questions over a woman's competence to perform in male-typed roles. In contrast to the impact of descriptive stereotypes, the consequence of breaking prescriptive stereotypes is a negative evaluation of the individual as a person rather than a negative evaluation of their competence – it becomes personal, in other words. When a woman behaves in a manner that neglects gender prescriptions she is likely to encounter some form of backlash and penalty[3–5] not just by men but by other women as well. These penalties appear to occur only when women are successful in roles that are considered to be male.[6]

Prescriptive stereotypes contain both Shoulds and Should Nots. Shoulds include an expectation that someone will behave in a way consistent with the gender stereotype. So, for example, women should be caring and warm. When a woman fails to behave in the prescribed way there are penalties; so when a woman chooses not to help a colleague she will be evaluated more negatively than a man who chooses not to help. This is because there is a prescribed stereotype, an expectation, that women *should* help. When a man fails to display helping behaviours at work he is less likely to be penalised, since such behaviour is not stereotypically expected of him.

Conversely, when a woman does help others, this is more likely to go unremarked since this is the expected norm, whereas a man displaying the same behaviours will be rewarded. Absence of the behaviour is noted for women, but the presence of it is not.[7] This is not a "swings and roundabouts" situation – it is more like swings and swings.

For a woman, the Should Nots encompass behaving in a way that is stereotypically male. For example, when a woman displays traits of agency such as assertiveness and decisiveness, she is acting against the prescribed stereotype for her gender.

Both Shoulds and Should Nots are pervasive, powerful and act to uphold the status quo. The Shoulds serve to maintain the beliefs that currently exist. The Should Nots help to reinforce boundaries and eliminate the possibility of grey areas.

The consequences of violating the Shoulds and Should Nots

As shown in Table 4.1, breaking these rules results in reduced liking, social acceptance and influence.[8] Communicating directly and clearly is something that is desirable in a leader. However, women who communicate in this manner are less able to influence male listeners than women who spoke in a more tentative, mitigating style.[9] Acting against prescription leads to a combination of emotional and social exclusion. Women who display the traits associated with the male stereotype are seen as being less socially appealing.[10]

Table 4.1: Summary of the consequences of violating prescriptive stereotypes.

Consequences	Impact
Reduced social acceptance and liking Seen as cold, selfish, devious, hostile and a poor team-mate	Less likely to be hired Reduced influence Increased sexism

Reduced liking and influence can have significant repercussions in the workplace, including lower performance ratings[11–13] and salary recommendations,[6] and reduced access to social networks[14] and special career opportunities.[6]

This topic is particularly important since there has been a move over recent years to focus not just on *what* a person does (i.e. their competence) but on *how* they do it (i.e. their interpersonal effectiveness). This creates a double bind for professional women, in that they are less likely to be seen as successful on both of the required dimensions. They can be interpersonally effective, displaying communal traits, but not deemed as competent, or they can be competent but not interpersonally effective. It's a classic lose–lose situation, made all the worse by being presented as an advance on a blinkered competency-based approach.

For example, a constant criticism of Hillary Clinton when she ran for the Democratic nomination for President of the United States was that she was too cold, too ambitious and too hard. Then, famously, she became tearful at a press conference and was suddenly seen as too emotional to be considered as a serious leadership contender. Others believed her tears were produced only for the press and public, thereby confirming the perception of her as calculating.

Fig 4.1: Hillary Clinton.

Fig 4.2: Julia Gillard.

Politicians are regularly lampooned, but the level of criticism of some high-profile women in politics goes well beyond normal levels of satire. With Julia Gillard, for example, the former Australian premier, everything – including her size, dress sense, personality and toughness – all came under the most intense scrutiny, with political opponents and journalists alike describing her in the most sexist terms.

The attitude that women are not expected to participate in the public realm dates back for centuries, and we have only to look at the treatment doled out to female politicians to see that these beliefs are still alive and well today.

A female senior executive we met recently told us about the difficulty she was experiencing with her boss. They were discussing the company's strategy and she disagreed very strongly about one aspect of it and made her views very clear. Finally and in exasperation he told her to "stop adopting these intellectually superior positions"! This incident inaugurated a period of coolness towards her which in turn has discouraged her from disagreeing with him again. This leader's behaviour towards dissenting men is very different. He is publicly committed to diversity, but unaware of the different ways in which he responds to the men and women in his team. The female senior manager told us she feels she cannot be herself at work because she constantly has to think about how a critical comment will be received. She is second-guessing how she ought to behave, which undermines her own performance. She has even been asked by another team member why she has started to be over-admiring of the leader.

Not behaving according to prescribed social norms can also bring penalties for men. Until recently, this area of research had been little explored.[15] For men, being passive,[16] exhibiting emotional self-disclosure[17] and being successful in feminine domains have been found to invoke penalties.

Even being modest for a man carries a penalty. Recent research explored what happened when men exhibited modesty in job-hiring situations. Stereotypically, the expectation is that men will self-promote. When men acted modestly they were less liked than women acting modestly.[18]

In recent years we have seen more men opting to stay at home to be the primary childcare provider, or scaling back their work hours in order to enable a more equal distribution of career investment within the household. Shared parental leave exists in some countries and is being discussed in many more, so the options are opening up for men in a way that has previously not been possible. Whether or not such opportunities are taken up is likely to rest largely on whether the prescriptions faced by men change as well. Without such shifts in thought, the traditional pressures on men and women are likely to remain the same.

While policies may be changing to enable more equality at work, mindsets are not.[19] Consequently, men will continue to be expected to display a high level of agency. The expectation that men will be successful, powerful and dominant[20] is relatively stable and likely to remain. Men experience backlash effects when they carry out what is seen as women's work. Pressure to adhere to masculine ideals has been shown to impact men's mental and physical health[21] and their relationships.[22] This study, along with the others we have referenced, also shows the way that the same behaviour displayed by men and women will be assessed differently depending on the direction of the prescription. There are penalties for going against a stereotype and rewards for conforming to it.

Crossing these invisible boundaries triggers penalties. The existence of such penalties – which may be subtle but are always emotionally effective – discourages people from repeating their transgressive behaviour in future situations. Both genders are under great pressure to conform to gender-specific behavioural norms.

For example, a woman who displays assertiveness as a personal assistant (PA) will be highly valued. A major part of a PA's role is to protect her charge, so acting assertively can be a way of defending and enhancing his (and it usually is "his") inaccessibility. However, a woman who displays the same assertiveness in a role traditionally associated with men will be frowned upon and encounter social sanctions. A female executive will be seen to be being "pushy" or "strident" if she behaves assertively – even though assertiveness would seem to go with the role, not the sex of the person in the role.

For a heterosexual couple, where both partners are violating gender norms, the consequences are likely to be even more extreme. Both the man and woman are likely to experience backlash and penalties for behaving in ways inconsistent with their expected gender norms. Both parties may encounter obstacles to job opportunities, career progression and salary, landing a double whammy on the household.

Prescriptive stereotypes and sexism

Prescriptive stereotypes and sexism are related because both are likely to be motivationally driven and serve as a means to maintain the status differences between men and women, keeping women in the inferior position. Sexism doesn't have to be obvious or overt to be corrosive.

While sexism has traditionally been seen as expressed negativity towards women, Glick and Fiske[23] were the first to assert that sexism takes different forms, namely *hostility*, *benevolence* and *ambivalence*, with each form leading to different behaviours. Unlike other prejudices, sexism is unique in that both positive and negative thoughts towards women can exist simultaneously.

The definition of hostile sexism is akin to Allport's[24] definition of ethnic prejudice: "prejudice is an antipathy based upon a faulty and inflexible generalisation." Hostile sexists will view a woman positively on work-related dimensions, such as problem solving, but describe her as "aggressive, selfish, greedy and cold", thereby attacking her personal traits.[25]

Glick and Fiske[23] define benevolent sexism as:

> A set of interrelated attitudes toward women that are sexist in terms of viewing women stereotypically and in restricted roles but that are subjectively positive in feeling tone (for the perceiver) and also tend to elicit behaviours typically categorised as pro-social (e.g. helping) or intimacy-seeking (e.g. self-disclosure).

In essence, benevolence flatters a woman on traits she is expected to exhibit while reinforcing her inferiority and suggesting her dependence on men.[26] Its subtle nature as well as the flattery involved means it is less likely to be noticed.[27]

The level of a man's sexism is likely to influence his behaviour when interacting with women. For example, men with higher levels of sexism have been found to write using more sexist language than less sexist men[28] and are less likely to view making unwanted sexual advances as sexist.[29]

The behaviours associated with hostile and benevolent sexism differ and the presence of each will depend on the role the woman is perceived to take in society. Hostile sexism is more likely to be present towards a woman when she is operating in a non-traditional role, whereas benevolent sexism is usually observed when the female is in a traditional role.[30] The final outcomes, however – such as discrimination and reduced access to opportunity – may be the same. Both types of sexism aim to maintain the status quo.

Context is important in most things, as we have seen, and the same consideration applies to the impact of sexist behaviour. When a woman was on the receiving end of sexist behaviour from a male her performance on tasks was diminished, but only when the tasks were traditionally associated with an area in which men excel, such as engineering and maths. When females met with males who exhibited low levels of sexism they performed as well as men.[31] This shows how interpersonal interactions can subtly impact performance, and how vital it is to take a look at the environment within which women work.

Benevolent sexism could be seen as more positive and less harmful than hostile sexism. But let's be clear: it is just as dangerous in its impact on women. In fact, benevolent sexism may have a *greater* impact on a woman's cognitive performance than hostile sexism.[26]

Hostile sexism is often easy to identify due to the clear expression of not liking or valuing a woman because of her gender. And because hostile sexism can be attributed to an external source,[26] that of the person displaying it, it is less likely to have an impact on performance. The meaning behind benevolent comments is often ambiguous and therefore difficult to label as sexism. Indeed, we have often heard women convey their uncertainly at comments aimed at them: was the person just being polite or was there some hidden meaning behind the compliment? For some reason, the comment didn't feel right, but it's hard to put a finger on any overt offensive content.

It is this very uncertainty that leads to self-doubt and diverts mental energy away from focusing on the task at hand.[26] With our working memory distracted by trying to process and understand such comments, task performance is negatively impacted. Derdene and his colleagues[26] found that, while females were less likely to perceive benevolent sexism as sexism, they did find it unpleasant. Those who had been on the receiving end of benevolent sexism performed more poorly than those exposed to no sexism or hostile sexism. Another study found that even the mere suggestion from a peer that an instructor was sexist could impact a woman's test performance.[32]

Benevolent sexism therefore has a greater negative impact.

Neither are the two forms of sexism mutually exclusive. We are perfectly capable of holding both forms of sexism at the same time, which then leads to its third manifestation as ambivalent sexism.[23] At times, a person may show displays of hostile sexism and at other times display benevolence.[23,33] Situational factors play a key role in determining which form of sexism will be displayed. For example, when encountering female professionals and women in non-traditional roles, an individual is more likely to display hostile sexism. The same person may then display benevolent sexism when interacting with women who are homemakers or who occupy traditional roles.

Although there were no gender differences in ambivalent sexism – women as well as men can be sexist – men's sexism was more motivationally driven than women's as a result of greater acceptance of social norms. Women's reduced acceptance of such norms in recent years may explain why we are now seeing gender differences emerge on explicit measures of sexism.[34] Beneath the surface, however, the genders may be more similar than they appear.

Anti-discrimination laws may have created a major decline in overt discrimination, but more subtle forms of discrimination have developed.[35] These take the form of interpersonal behaviours that either reward or punish women when they stay within or step outside traditional roles and are akin to hostile or benevolent sexism.

In a field experiment,[36] visibly pregnant and non-pregnant confederates either applied for sales jobs (a non-traditional role) or acted as customers (a traditional female role). Overt and subtle discrimination were both measured; the former by factors such as permission to complete a job application and job call-backs; the latter by observing incidences of hostile and benevolent behaviour including body language. The researchers actually found no differences in overt discrimination. However, pregnant women received more hostility in interpersonal behaviours when pursuing non-traditional roles (the sales job) and more benevolence when pursuing traditional roles (the customer). Interestingly, no gender differences were found among the assessors: men and women both showed a bias against pregnant women. We have learned how we ought to behave when confronted with someone who does not meet our expectations but, despite our attempts to control ourselves, our attitudes and beliefs find expression in other ways.

Ambivalent sexism can also find expression in the way we choose to reward someone. In one study when women received patronising feedback, defined as excessive praise for their work, in place of a tangible reward, their task performance was diminished, whereas the performance of men was not. What's interesting here is how gender prescriptions may have influenced subsequent behaviour. Men are required to be competitive and fight against injustices, whereas women are expected to be timid and weak. It may well have been the fulfilment of these expectations that led to the differences in subsequent task performance.[36] In any case, it is clear that praising the capabilities of a woman through a performance review but not giving her a tangible reward such as a promotion or pay rise could hinder her future performance. Ambivalent sexism may be at play in workplaces more than we would like to believe. On the one hand, a woman may be praised for her performance (benevolence) while at the same time she is paid less and opportunities are withheld from her (hostility).

All forms of sexism prescribe how the relationship between men and women should be and serve to maintain men's superior status. As such, prescriptive stereotypes about how men and women should differ are likely to be motivationally driven. This is an important point, and one that we will return to later, since it has implications for how gender discrimination should be addressed.

The subtle tyranny of context

Arguments over whether men and women have essentially different traits are, from an objective point of view, irrelevant. The only relevance to perceived gender differences is their social reception. When we say that someone is acting in a feminine way, we are saying they are acting in a way *designated* as feminine. The same goes for masculine behaviour. The differences are apparent, but socially constructed. That is, they are not real differences, but since we believe they are, they function in that way.

While the stereotypes we all hold are remarkably crude, they are also very elusive. This is because they shift in aspect depending on context.

Kevin Tang collected eight pieces of research that overturn gender stereotypes:[37]

- Before they go to school, boys show more emotions than girls do.

- Boys are no better than girls at maths, right around the world.

- Young men are more emotionally affected by relationship problems than young women.

- Men buy and sell shares less rationally than women.

- Men can read emotional cues as well as women.

- Men check on their partners online more than women do – a proxy for jealous behaviour.

- Divorced men are twice as likely to commit suicide than divorced women – and men are already twice as likely to commit suicide anyway.

- When playing anonymously, women are more aggressive at online games than men.

Some of these counterintuitive results are revealed by careful measurement, others by alteration of context. It's possible to learn that girls and boys are equally good at maths by giving them maths tests, and to assess emotional literacy by showing women and men clips of people expressing various emotions. The contextual shifts are perhaps more interesting. Revelation by measurement shows that we haven't been testing our assumptions, but contextual shifting shows that the environment or background to a gender effect is just as (maybe more) powerful as the explicit content of the stereotype in action.

Take the example of young boys' emotional displays. Measurement tells us something surprising about preschoolers. But the shift from home to school environment tells us that girls and boys learn to emote in line with expectations because of the institutional setting.

Similarly, women are not "supposed" to like aggressive gameplay. Remove their feminine identity in the game, and they will blow the bad guys away with even more relish than men. Anonymity reveals an essential equality here, just as institutionalisation by school distorts another essential equality.

The powerful influence of context on the emergence of difference is further demonstrated by differences in maths ability often observed between the sexes:

- In Grades 2 through to 11 there are no gender differences on standardised maths tests in school.[38]

- However, in high school boys do start to outperform girls at complex problem-solving.[39,40]

- At the same time, relationships between boys and girls begin to shift. It's around this time that boys start to show more of a sexual interest in girls.

- In addition, girls come to see themselves as women to whom stereotypes about women's maths ability apply.[41]

- At high school, then, there is a shift in boys' behaviour towards girls which may trigger social identity threat. This may be the reason underlying gender differences in maths performance that emerge at this time.[31]

One way to understand this problem is to examine how contexts are constructed and to see if they can be altered. As we have seen, we categorise quickly and decisively, using as few categories as we can get away with. We do the same when we categorise contexts, often failing to notice that a single social situation usually contains many overlapping but different contexts, depending on the individuals involved, their power relationships with each other and the wider setting of the situation.

In a period spanning over sixty years, Jean Twenge[42] found that American women's assertiveness rose and fell in line with their social status. Broadly speaking, women's self-reports on assertiveness and dominance scales increased between 1931 and 1945, decreased between 1946 and 1967, and increased between 1968 to 1993, the endpoint of the meta-analyses. Twenge also reported that samples taken since that time show women's assertiveness scores increasing further, so that many recent samples show no sex differences at all.

It would be easy to take data from one period and assume that this describes the levels of assertiveness in men and women. It would be too easy to state that these differences are natural and innate. But this research shows something else entirely. By correlating the self-esteem measures with social indicators such as educational level and age at first marriage, Twenge confirmed that assertiveness varies with status and role so that the societal changes that occur around us, actually become part of us in the form of a personality trait.[1] In other words, you become your context.

Research shows that when working in same-sex groups on a gender-neutral task, men and women do not differ in participation and task suggestions[43,44] or in their acceptance of influence from others.[45] But when teams are composed of both men and women, differences in behaviour emerge. When the task is stereotypically male then men will be more influential and assertive, but when the task is perceived to be feminine it is women who are more assertive and influential.[46,47] We conform to the gender promptings of the task. This shows that, as well as recognising the gender of people, we are adept at reading the gender of activities.

In mixed gender groups, men have – or take – an advantage: they talk more,[48] use less tentative language,[47] use assertive gestures to display dominance,[49] make more suggestions[50] and have more influence than women.[9] Observing men performing "better" in mixed groups, we infer that men *are* "better" than women in such situations. We may also infer that the group would perform better if male domination was acknowledged, or if women were excluded.

Our different expectations about men and women give rise to observed differences in behaviour. But these differences in behaviour are generated by our expectations, not by supposed gender differences. Our expectations, in turn, are thought to rest on beliefs about status.

Status beliefs govern who we expect to exercise authority in a given situation. When someone who is not expected to assert authority does so, our status beliefs are defied and our behaviour expectations activated. We resist the person's claims of authority and penalise them for stepping out of line. This is a common reaction to women in leadership positions. It's not just that they don't belong; they are not good enough to belong.

Men and women can behave identically, but the context of their behaviour will influence whether the behaviour is displayed, suppressed, accepted or punished.

When a woman asserts authority in mixed gender or male-associated contexts, she is likely to experience one or more forms of social backlash which will hinder her ability to lead others. Such women are disliked, perceived as less trustworthy and have less influence over men compared to men or less assertive women.

We were asked to look at the experiences of men and women in a large accountancy firm and in particular to focus on why there were so few female partners and directors. One of the factors that emerged was the way in which the same behaviours were labelled differently depending on whether it was a male or female displaying them. Leaders are expected to be agentic: to get things done, take control, set direction. When a man acted in this way he was seen as assertive, focused and strategic. A woman behaving in this fashion was seen as aggressive, pushy and, worst of all, behaving like a man. The same actions are seen as a positive in one gender and negative in the other.

It is generally accepted, for example, that people need to "play the game" if they wish to succeed in organisations. This involves networking and the allied art of self-promotion. When researching the partner process in a professional services firm, Kumra and Vinnicombe[51] found that in order to progress to partner level there was a belief that consultants must promote their own achievements. This was something that the women in the study reported they did not feel comfortable doing. They felt they were disadvantaged by this requirement. Such nervousness is not surprising, given the wealth of research showing that when a woman self-promotes her competence she experiences social sanctions such as being less liked and deemed as less hireable.[5] Such subtle cues from the environment are bound to discourage women from self-promoting. On the other hand, self-promoting behaviour is congruent with male gender stereotypes and so, when it is deemed necessary for promotion, men have a distinct advantage.

Prescription and motivation

In summary, even when women prove their competence in action, prescriptive stereotypes kick in and have a very potent impact. While she has proved she can do a man's job, the woman is now behaving in a way that violates prescribed norms. She is behaving in a way that she should not, leading to penalties in the workplace.

We might expect that, once a woman has shown that she can perform as well as a man, the problem would disappear and there would be more equality in the workplace. The evidence of our eyes should trump the rules in our heads. This is the approach Davies takes in his report and recommendations. He approaches discrimination against women as a purely mathematical issue, believing that having more women at the top will solve the problem by changing the status quo and so leading to their acceptance in these roles.

This view neglects the powerful influence of prescriptive stereotypes. Even when we break away from stereotypes of how men and women are supposed to be different, we still need to overcome the beliefs surrounding what a woman should and shouldn't do.

The common thread in prescriptive stereotypes is motivational underpinning. Their purpose is to maintain the status quo. Where prescriptive stereotypes are in play, those who conform to the prescribed expectations are rewarded, whereas those who violate them are sanctioned.[52]

While there is overwhelming evidence that there are no differences between men and women and that descriptive stereotypes can be robustly refuted, the issue of prescriptive stereotyping remains. Our ideals about what men and women should do and how they should behave are complex and strongly influenced by context and situational factors. One thing that is clear, however, is that our ideals are strongly motivationally driven. We are keen to hold on to our beliefs and may hotly dispute anything that challenges them if maintaining the status quo has a pay-off for us personally. So while overcoming descriptive stereotypes is likely to involve raising awareness of unconscious bias and conducting some reprogramming of our beliefs and associations, changing prescriptive stereotypes is likely to require an entirely different approach.

A deeper look at individual differences will be required to tackle their influence. For example, how do people react when given feedback on their biases? Are they motivated to change them, or do they flatly deny them?

Although the content of gender stereotypes does not differ between the sexes, men are more likely to hold prescriptive gender stereotypes than women and report these explicitly.[52] As result, there is likely to be much higher conscious awareness of prescribed gender stereotypes: people are likely to have some insight into their beliefs about what men and women should be doing in society. This means that awareness-raising strategies, which are effective for diminishing the impact of descriptive gender stereotypes, are likely to prove ineffective against overcoming prescriptive stereotyping.

How can we combat prescriptive stereotypes? One approach is to examine a person's motivation to respond to bias once they have become aware of it. Motivation is a powerful individual difference that appears to indicate how much a person will be both disturbed by their biases and act in a way to address them. Merely raising awareness of their existence is unlikely to prove effective. According to Devine and colleagues[53] reduction of prejudice is a multi-step process. One crucial step is having a desire not to respond in a biased manner once you are aware of your biases. Accordingly, those with higher internal motivation not to be prejudiced exhibit lower levels of bias[53,54] and are more willing to engage in strategies to overcome their bias.[55] Future interventions therefore need to consider individual motivation to overcome bias if they are to have a broader impact on discrimination.

The prescriptions about what is acceptable behaviour for men and women at work are age-old and endure in today's workplace. Social context influences both acceptance and recognition of behaviour. We are socialised to regard certain styles of interaction or presentation as appropriate for various settings. On the other side of the equation, we associate these settings with a dominant gender. Sanctions act to reinforce stereotypes, encouraging people to behave according to prescribed gender norms and to reassert the idea that men and women are different.

References

1. Available at: http://skepticsannotatedbible.com. Accessed 23 September 2013.

2. Glick P, Fiske ST. 'Sexism and other "isms": Independence, status, and the ambivalent content of stereotypes.' In Swann WB Jr, Langlois JH and Gilbert LA (eds) *Sexism and Stereotypes in Modern Society: The Gender Science of Janet Taylor Spence*. American Psychological Association; 1999, pp. 193–221. doi: 10.1037/10277-008.

3. Rudman LA, Fairchild K. 'Reactions to counter-stereotypic behavior: The role of backlash in cultural stereotype maintenance.' *Journal of Personality and Social Psychology* 2004; 87 (2): 157–176. doi:10.1037/0022-3514.87.2.157.

4. Rudman LAL, Glick PP. 'Feminized management and backlash toward agentic women: The hidden costs to women of a kinder, gentler image of middle managers.' *Journal of Personality and Social Psychology* 1999; 77(5): 1004–1010. doi:10.1037/0022-3514.77.5.1004.

5. Rudman LA, Glick P. 'Prescriptive gender stereotypes and backlash toward agentic women.' *Journal of Social Issues* 2002; 57(4): 743–762.

6. Heilman ME, Wallen AS, Fuchs D, Tamkins MM. 'Penalties for success: Reactions to women who succeed at male gender-typed tasks.' *Journal of Applied Psychology* 2004; 89(3): 416–427. doi:10.1037/0021-9010.89.3.416.

7. Heilman ME, Chen JJ. 'Same behavior, different consequences: Reactions to men's and women's altruistic citizenship behavior.' *Journal of Applied Psychology* 2005; 90(3): 431 –441. doi:10.1037/0021-9010.90.3.431.

8. Heilman ME, Parks-Stamm EJ. 'Gender stereotypes in the workplace: Obstacles to women's career progress.' *Advances in Group Processes* 2007; 24: 47–77. doi:10.1016/ S0882-6145(07)24003-2.3d.

9. Carli LL. 'Gender, language, and influence.' *Journal of Personality and Social Psychology* 1990; 59(5): 941–951. doi: 10.1037/0022-3514.59.5.941.

10. Rudman LAL. 'Self-promotion as a risk factor for women: the costs and benefits of counter-stereotypical impression management.' *Journal of Personality and Social Psychology* 1998; 74(3): 629–645. doi:10.1037/0022-3514.74.3.629.

11. Dipboye RL. 'Some neglected variables in research on discrimination in appraisals.' *The Academy of Management Review Archive* 1985; 10(1): 116–127.

12. Feldman JM, Lynch JG. 'Self-generated validity and other effects of measurement on belief, attitude, intention, and behavior.' *Journal of Applied Psychology* 1988; 73(3): 421.

13. Ilgen DR, Feldman JM. 'Performance appraisal: A process focus.' *Research in Organizational Behavior* 1983; 5: 141–197.

14. Casciaro TT, Lobo MSM. 'Competent jerks, lovable fools, and the formation of social networks.' *Harvard Business Review* 2005; 83(6): 92–149.

15. Heilman ME, Eagly AH. 'Gender stereotypes are alive, well, and busy producing workplace discrimination.' *Industrial and Organizational Psychology* 2008; 1(4): 393–398.

16. Costrich N, Feinstein J, Kidder L, Marecek J, Pascale L. 'When stereotypes hurt: Three studies of penalties for sex-role reversals.' *Journal of Experimental Social Psychology* 1975; 11(6): 520–530.

17. Derlega VJ, Chaikin AL. 'Norms affecting self-disclosure in men and women.' *Journal of Consulting and Clinical Psychology* 1976; 44(3): 376.

18. Moss-Racusin CA, Phelan JE, Rudman LA. 'When men break the gender rules: Status incongruity and backlash against modest men.' *Psychology of Men & Masculinity* 2010; 11(2): 140–151. doi:10.1037/a0018093.

19. Diekman AB, Goodfriend W, Goodwin S. 'Dynamic stereotypes of power: Perceived change and stability in gender hierarchies.' *Sex Roles* 2004; 50(3-4): 201–215.

20. Kimmel MS. *The Gendered Society*. Oxford University Press; 2004.

21. Courtenay WH. 'Engendering health: A social constructionist examination of men's health beliefs and behaviors.' *Psychology of Men & Masculinity* 2000; 1(1): 4–15. doi:10.1037//1524-9220.1.1.4.

22. Burn SM, Ward AZ. 'Men's conformity to traditional masculinity and relationship satisfaction.' *Psychology of Men & Masculinity* 2005; 6(4): 254–263. doi:10.1037/1524-9220.6.4.254.

23. Glick P, Fiske ST. 'The ambivalent sexism inventory: Differentiating hostile and benevolent sexism.' *Journal of Personality and Social Psychology* 1996; 70(3): 491.

24. Allport GW. *The Nature of Prejudice*. Addison-Wesley; 1954.

25. Glick P, Diebold J, Bailey-Werner B, Zhu L. 'The two faces of Adam: Ambivalent sexism and polarized attitudes toward women.' *Personality and Social Psychology Bulletin* 1997; 23(12): 1323–1334. doi:10.1177/01461672972312009.

26. Dardenne B, Dumont M, Bollier T. 'Insidious dangers of benevolent sexism: Consequences for women's performance.' *Journal of Personality and Social Psychology* 2007; 93(5): 764–779. doi:10.1037/0022-3514.93.5.764.

27. Barreto M, Ellemers N. 'The burden of benevolent sexism: how it contributes to the maintenance of gender inequalities.' *European Journal of Social Psychology* 2005; 35(5): 633–642. doi:10.1002/ejsp.270.

28. Swim JK, Mallett R, Stangor C. 'Understanding subtle sexism: Detection and use of sexist language.' *Sex Roles* 2004; 51(3-4): 117–128.

29. Swim JK, Mallett R, Russo-Devosa Y. 'Judgments of sexism: A comparison of the subtlety of sexism measures and sources of variability in judgments of sexism.' *Psychology of Women Quarterly* 2005; 29(4): 406–411.

30. Cuddy AJC, Fiske ST, Glick P. 'When professionals become mothers, warmth doesn't cut the ice.' *Journal of Social Issues* 2004; 60(4): 701–718.

31. Logel C, Walton GM, Spencer SJ, Iserman EC, Hippel von W, Bell AE. 'Interacting with sexist men triggers social identity threat among female engineers.' *Journal of Personality and Social Psychology* 2009; 96(6): 1089–1103. doi:10.1037/a0015703.

32. Adams G, Garcia DM, Purdie-Vaughns V, Steele CM. 'The detrimental effects of a suggestion of sexism in an instruction situation.' *Journal of Experimental Social Psychology* 2006; 42(5): 602–615. doi:10.1016/j.jesp.2005.10.004.

33. Glick P, Fiske ST. 'An ambivalent alliance: Hostile and benevolent sexism as complementary justifications for gender inequality.' *American Psychologist* 2001; 56(2): 109. doi:10.1037//0003-066X.56.2.109.

34. Eagly AH, Makhijani MG, Klonsky BG. 'Gender and the evaluation of leaders: A meta-analysis.' *Psychological Bulletin* 1992; 111: 3–22.

35. Hebl MR, King EB, Glick P, Singletary SL, Kazama S. 'Hostile and benevolent reactions toward pregnant women: Complementary interpersonal punishments and rewards that maintain traditional roles.' *Journal of Applied Psychology* 2007; 92(6): 1499–1511. doi:10.1037/0021-9010.92.6.1499.

36. Vescio TK, Gervais SJ, Snyder M, Hoover A. 'Power and the creation of patronizing environments: The stereotype-based behaviors of the powerful and their effects on female performance in masculine domains.' *Journal of Personality and Social Psychology* 2005; 88(4): 658–672. doi:10.1037/0022-3514.88.4.658.

37. Available at: http://www.buzzfeed.com/kevintang/8-studies-that-debunk-male-stereotypes. Accessed 23 September 2013.

38. Hyde JS, Lindberg SM, Linn MC, Ellis AB, Williams CC. 'Diversity. Gender similarities characterize math performance.' *Science* 2008; 321(5888): 494–495. doi:10.1126/science.1160364.

39. Hyde JS, Fennema E, Lamon SJ. 'Gender differences in mathematics performance: a meta-analysis.' *Psychological Bulletin* 1990; 107(2): 139–155.

40. Hyde JS, Linn MC. 'Gender similarities in mathematics and science.' *Science* 2006; 314: 599–600.

41. Steele J. 'Children's gender stereotypes about math: The role of stereotype stratification.' *Journal of Applied Social Psychology* 2003; 33(12): 2587–2606.

42. Twenge JMJ. 'Changes in women's assertiveness in response to status and roles: a cross-temporal meta-analysis, 1931–1993.' *Journal of Personality and Social Psychology* 2001; 81(1): 133–145. doi:10.1037/0022-3514.81.1.133.

43. Johnson C, Clay-Warner J, Funk SJ. 'Effects of authority structures and gender on interaction in same-sex task groups.' *Social Psychology Quarterly* 1996; 59(3): 221–236.

44. Shelly RK, Munroe PT. 'Do women engage in less task behavior than men?' *Sociological Perspectives* 1999; 42(1): 49–67.

45. Pugh MD, Wahrman R. 'Neutralizing sexism in mixed-sex groups: Do women have to be better than men?' *American Journal of Sociology* 1983; 88(4): 746–762.

46. Wagner DG, Berger J. 'Gender and interpersonal task behaviors: Status expectation accounts.' *Sociological Perspectives* 1997; 40(1): 1–32.

47. Dovidio JF, Brown CE, Heltman K. 'Power displays between women and men in discussions of gender-linked tasks: A multichannel study.' *Journal of Personality* 1988; 55(4): 580–587.

48. James D, Drakich J. 'Understanding gender differences in amount of talk: A critical review of research.' In Tannen D (ed.), *Gender and Conversational Interaction*. Oxford University Press; 1993, pp. 281–312.

49. Ellyson SL, Dovidio JF, Brown CE. 'The look of power: Gender differences and similarities in visual dominance behavior.' In Ridgeway C (ed.), *Gender, Interaction, and Inequality*. Springer; 1992, pp. 50–80.

50. Wood WW, Karten SJS. 'Sex differences in interaction style as a product of perceived sex differences in competence.' *Journal of Personality and Social Psychology* 1986; 50(2): 341–347. doi:10.1037/0022-3514.50.2.341.

51. Kumra S, Vinnicombe S. 'A study of the promotion to partner process in a professional services firm: How women are disadvantaged.' *British Journal of Management* 2008; 19 (s1): S65–S74. doi:10.1111/j.1467-8551.2008.00572.x.

52. Burgess D, Borgida E. 'Who women are, who women should be: Descriptive and prescriptive gender stereotyping in sex discrimination.' *Psychology, Public Policy, and Law* 1999; 5(3): 665–692. doi:10.1037//1076-8971.5.3.665.

53. Devine PG, Plant EA, Amodio DM, Harmon-Jones E, Vance SL. 'The regulation of explicit and implicit race bias: The role of motivations to respond without prejudice.' *Journal of Personality and Social Psychology* 2002; 82(5): 835–848. doi:10.1037//0022-3514.82.5.835.

54. Klonis SC. 'Internal and external motivation to respond without sexism.' *Personality and Social Psychology Bulletin* 2005; 31(9): 1237–1249. doi:10.1177/0146167205275304.

55. Plant EA, Devine PG, Cox WTL, et al. 'The Obama effect: Decreasing implicit prejudice and stereotyping.' *Journal of Experimental Social Psychology* 2009; 45(4): 961–964. doi:10.1016/j.jesp.2009.04.018.

5

TAKE ME TO YOUR LEADER: PROTOTYPES IN ACTION

What is a leader? There are numerous definitions of leadership, and limited agreement about what it is actually is. At the time of writing, Google offers around 96,400 answers. One of a thousand or more of the definitions in that ocean of information may well be correct. Many will be contradictory, like the beginning of this website:

> A leader is someone who people choose to follow: PERIOD.
> A leader influences others to do things that they may not otherwise do.

Further down the list, we're told: "Ideally, the effective leader is a person of integrity."[1]

While explicit descriptions of what a good leader looks like vary considerably, there is evidence that we have very well established prototypes, or implicit theories, that are remarkably consistent across people. Definitions aside, none of these answers is likely to be the most truthful and used one. Dear reader, a leader is a man.

Recognising ourselves as the machinery of stereotyping comes close to one of Jung's theories that people are influenced by *archetypes*: unconscious ideas that we inherit from our forebears. They are a kind of cultural heritage that we all unknowingly carry and act upon. Each archetype is thought to be the original from which a series of copies may be struck. The idea of printing – and imprinting – is there, but here we have a sense of natural origins and universal application, rather than the business interests of a publisher.

Some philosophers also talk about *exemplars*, which are typical instances of a class.[2] So, we might think about a *dog* by imagining what we take to be a typical dog: four legs, barking, tail wagging. In reality, dogs come in all shapes and sizes, but it's easier to use the exemplar in normal thought.

But do these terminological distinctions matter? Yes. Each of these forms of idea influences how we think and behave. Knowing where they come from, and their relative credibility, empowers us to reject, replace or modify them.

Knowing that an idea is based on an archetype will tell us that some fundamental human value is being appealed to. If we are using a prototype, we can ask which goals the prototype was designed to serve. Knowing that we are using an exemplar will remind us that we're working with rough ideas derived from the most salient common features of a class, and are most likely ignoring the variability in the real population we are thinking about. If we are acting according to a stereotype, we can remember that the force of this particular idea is mere repetition.

As we have seen, organisations were created and designed by men to suit men, established by American engineers in the late nineteenth and early twentieth centuries. Organisations are gendered, and this has an impact on how they are structured and managed, what is valued and what is expected. It also has an impact on the way we view leaders and leadership.

And it is not just men who think this either.

The IAT (Implicit Association Test), the highly respected test of unconscious biases, shows women are as biased towards male leaders as men are. Although the explicit attitudes of women are more egalitarian,[3,4,5] their implicit attitudes

126

are the same.[6] The very nature of implicit processes means that we are often unaware of their presence and the influence they have on our judgements and behaviour, operating as they do automatically when required without conscious effort.

Our leadership prototypes, also known as implicit leadership theories,[7] are belief systems thought to be formed early in our lives and stored in our long-term memory. They are systems that enable us to distinguish the features and traits of leaders from non-leaders.

Take a look at these eight distinct factors of implicit leadership theories: sensitivity, dedication, tyranny, charisma, attractiveness, masculinity, intelligence and strength.[8] Notice anything? Of these eight traits associated with leadership, at least six, and possibly seven, are stereotypically masculine. We therefore possess theories of leadership that match male gender stereotypes.[9,10,11] It is therefore not surprising that when we think "leader" we also think "male". This leads to the assumption that women are not suited for these jobs and will have a higher risk of failing, and as a result employment decisions are likely to be unfavourable.[12] The sheer weight of research demonstrating this effect is very difficult to ignore.[9,13,14]

The fact that most senior leaders seen in everyday life are male merely confirms the prototype stored in our collective long-term memory. Workplaces don't just respond to and reflect prevailing ideas of gender – they also produce and promote them. Organisations are a potent source of information that can be used to strengthen stereotypes, as well as being important amplifiers of entrenched attitudes. While we tend to see organisations as economic engines, or as social settings, they are also generators of meaning.

Research approaches and differences in leadership

When researchers find slight differences between men and women, how much do these differences matter? They seem to confirm the idea that males and females are innately different. If the sexes are innately different, then it is fair – and even obligatory – to look for gender differentiation in skills or preferences. However, it's an error to assume that some small experimental difference between men and women confirms the reality of gender categorisation. Trivial differences are often used to make sweeping generalisations.

The research looking at leadership styles can be placed into several categories:

- Academic
- Personality questionnaires
- 360-degree feedback
- Interviews.

Different results are found depending on the approach taken. Writers who advocate a difference between men's and women's leadership styles often draw on personal experiences of working in organisations. Such data is likely to contain severe distortions because, as we have seen, we habitually (mis) interpret information to ensure it matches our beliefs and expectations. Other evidence for a fundamental difference between male and female leadership includes informal surveys and interviews with managers.[15] This kind of data is also questionable. One key factor is the number of genders you expect to find operating in your survey population. Look for differences between women and men, and you will find (apparent) differences between women and men.

Academic research

Academic research, and by this we mean controlled experiments and field studies, finds overall that it is difficult to detect any meaningful differences between men and women. Those differences that are found tend to confirm the prescriptive views that we hold of the genders.

Any differences are also more likely to be found in laboratory studies than in the field. A student's ideas about leadership therefore may be more bound up with stereotypical views than the views of someone practising leadership for real.

In a literature review of over 80 studies, the researchers[16] found overall male and female leaders were equally effective. However, men and women were more effective in the "right" settings – men in male-oriented contexts, women in female-oriented contexts.[17] Effectiveness is therefore not just a matter of what you do, but where you do it.

Some professions and disciplines are informally regarded as primarily male or female. The military, for example, would seem to be male, while social work is female. There are of course women in the military and men in social work. Yet the stereotypical leader at the top levels of both domains is male.

Summing up the research on gender differences in leadership, the authors of the highly respected book, *Organisational Behaviour*, conclude:

> The evidence suggests that the best place to begin is with the recognition that there are few, if any, important differences between men and women that will affect their job performance. There are, for instance, no consistent male–female differences in problem-solving ability, analytical skills, competitive drive, motivation, sociability or learning agility. Psychological studies have found that women are more willing to conform and that men are more aggressive and more likely than women to have expectations of success, but those differences are minor.[18]

Commenting on a meta-analysis study which showed that the only differences between men and women were in motor performance (in particular, throwing distance and speed), the authors of *Work in the 21st Century* concluded:

> So unless leadership positions require the CEO to throw the quarterly report the length of the conference table, it would not appear that women have less potential than men to become managers and leaders.[19]

(It should be noted that the differences in levels of aggression are also now a subject of debate. Men are more aggressive than women but these differences, when compared to other species, are very small indeed.)

You want more? The British psychologists Stephen Woods and Michael West in their book *The Psychology of Work Organisations* noted that where differences are found in the leadership styles and role performance of men and women they are "so small in fact that it is safer to assume that there is no difference in leadership effectiveness between men and women".[20]

Personality questionnaires

Personality questionnaires typically present a number of statements about behaviour, beliefs and values. The respondent is asked to state the extent to which each statement is true of them. The results are therefore self-reported, but the statements are designed to be highly specific and the data is typically normed; that is, compared to a relevant population. In other words, such results are controlled, precise and reliable.

When we look at these valuable sources, we find that the data line up with the academic research. The few differences found are small. For example, an analysis by Saville Consulting of nearly 15,000 people who had taken the Wave personality questionnaire found no differences between men and women on 35 out of the 36 dimensions, and only a small difference for the remaining one.[21]

For a more comprehensive analysis we can turn to SHL, one of the world's leading and largest test publishers. The authors of the report, Eugene Burke and Ray Glennon,[22] mined their data on the OPQ (Occupational Personality Questionnaire) to look for a number of indicators, including the availability of talent, both now and in the future. They also looked at gender difference. The data set was huge: over one million people, or 1,118,197 to be precise. They found that only 1 in 15 people have the potential to be a senior leader and that there are no differences in leadership capability between men and women. However, as Table 5.1 shows, although women have the same potential as men they are seriously under-represented in leadership positions in every country.

There was nothing in the data to suggest that the stereotypes we have about men and women (men being more agentic and women more communal) were supported. That being the case, it is not surprising to find that there are no differences in leadership potential: "The supply of leadership potential is generally as strong for women as it is for men."

Table 5.1: Gender and leadership.

Leaders for today rank	Country	% men with capabilities of being a leader today	% women with capabilities of being a leader today	Differences in leaders for today (+% favour men, - % favour women)	% leadership roles held by men
1	China (Hong Kong)	13.5	13.3	0.2	67
2	Germany	12.7	14.0	- 1.3	87
3	UK	9.5	11.7	- 2.2	80
4	Australia	8.5	12.5	- 4.0	76
5	US	8.6	11.8	- 3.2	83
6	Switzerland	9.9	9.3	0.6	78
7	Canada	7.7	9.9	- 2.2	75
8	Japan	9.3	6.8	2.5	95
9	Singapore	9.7	8.0	1.7	77
10	New Zealand	6.7	9.6	- 2.9	72
11	Sweden	7.4	8.2	- 0.8	77
12	China (Taiwan)	7.6	6.8	0.8	73
13	France	6.6	6.4	0.2	76
14	Thailand	8.2	5.9	2.3	61
15	Finland	6.9	6.7	0.2	73
16	Belgium	6.6	6.2	0.4	79
17	Spain	6.3	6.4	-0.1	76
18	Turkey	5.1	8.3	- 3.2	69
19	Italy	5.5	5.5	0.0	64
20	South Africa	4.5	6.8	- 2.3	72
20	United Arab Emirates	5.0	6.5	- 1.5	85
22	Mexico	5.3	8.0	- 2.7	82
23	Denmark	4.5	6.1	- 1.6	85
24	Brazil	6.9	5.5	1.4	73
25	Norway	4.5	6.5	- 2.0	58
	Average	7.5	8.3	- 0.8	76

360-degree feedback and interview data

Once we move away from the more objective data, differences begin to be seen. For example, one company analysed 360-degree feedback from 14,000 leaders and managers in British organisations. Eighteen leadership competencies were examined. The results seem to confirm some of the more comforting ideas about gender at work – particularly the notion that men and women are different, but complementary:

> The "male leadership style" is strategic and visionary, while the "female leadership style" is more social. On one hand, this study highlights the general areas in which men and women need leadership development. However, on the other, it suggests that the natural styles of men and women are complementary. By creating a balance of both types of leadership, through board-level diversity, organisations can bring about peak performance.[23]

But "strategic and visionary" are not actually *styles* of leadership. They are competencies that can be demonstrated in a number of different ways. Someone could be strategic and visionary in a social way. The assertion is that in order to have leadership teams that are both "strategic and visionary" and "social" you need to have a mix of men and women. Men, in other words, cannot be social and women cannot be strategic and visionary. Now try saying that out loud in any gathering of business people and see what happens!

The implication of this position is that men are better leaders because of their relevant competencies, while women do not have competencies worth commenting on, only a style. Perhaps this is unfair, and there is indeed such a thing as a "strategic and visionary" style. If so, it might still be hard to distinguish this style from charisma, confidence or arrogance. It will definitely be difficult to separate the apparent exercise of the style from the expectations we hold about the context of its use.

The Saville Consulting research mentioned above looked at 360-degree feedback data as well as collecting personality scores. Although the personality data found only one, small, significant difference on 36 dimensions, the 360 data revealed many more differences which are in line with our stereotypes. Men and women do not see themselves as different, but when asked to review and comment upon someone else's performance, our preconceived ideas and attitudes impact on our assessments.

Interview data

Which description of a piece of a food sounds the healthier to you: 90% fat-free or 10% fat? Would you feel happier if a doctor told you that the operation you are about to undergo has a 90% survival rate or a 10% mortality rate? These are examples of what Daniel Kahneman calls *framing*.[24] Framing captures how choices about presentation evoke not only different responses but different emotions.

Research based on interviews shows the biggest differences in male and female perceptions because of this framing effect. The question is usually not, "What qualities do you have as a leader?" but, "What qualities do you bring as a female leader?"

The assumption is that there is a difference. In addition, being recognised as bringing something different to men is bound to have a certain appeal. This increasingly forms the basis of the argument for why women are needed in leadership, which in turn nicely tees up the demand for a business case.

A fascinating illustration of these beliefs is a piece of research conducted by IDDAS[25] where a number of female non-executive directors described the strengths they bring to the boardroom. Spot the perpetuation (and, consequently, the reinforcement of positive gender stereotypes) in the following:

> Women are less blunt, and therefore, in some ways, more effective. When you are a non-executive director, you are there to give advice and stop the company going off the rails (which happens relatively rarely!). You are talking finer shades of grey, and women are more gentle in their probing.

> Women may approach things in a different way. Women are better at spinning many plates and having wider responsibilities and therefore perspectives. They may ask about different areas, rather than only focusing on one area.

> Women understand people better and are not embarrassed to talk about the issues. Men are less prepared to talk about individuals' needs. They talk more about the business issues, and outcomes, and only then do they look at personnel, and reasons for particular performance.

Such research shows that the beliefs held about how men and women differ are deep within our social DNA and are often taken as truths. The report concludes that the qualities women bring to the boardroom, which by implication makes them different to men, are:

- Being well qualified for the roles

- Bringing a different perspective

- Being aware of group dynamics

- Being committed to the goals of the organisation rather than their own agenda

- Being less ego-driven

- Being adept at challenging in a non-threatening way

- Being energised and committed to the role.

Which is of course fantastic! And brilliant! And amazing! Except of course it doesn't say a lot about the egocentric, uncommitted, lazy, unqualified men they are forced to spend their time with in the boardroom. But then women are also good at teamwork and building relationships, so maybe they have ways of keeping the bunch of no-good bozos in line.

This line of thinking is of course highly questionable – if not downright wrong. In the foreword to the IDDAS report Lord Freeman, struggling to say something – anything – of any significance, remarks: "They [women] make an enormous contribution to their respective boards, which has nothing to do with gender." While inadvertently demonstrating that it is possible to be both sheepish and patronising at the same, he is also saying that men and women make the same contributions. No amount of wishful thinking is going to alter that.

It is this type of research that predominates in the popular media. But the data are flawed and so is the methodology. The fundamental problem with this kind of approach is the base assumption that there is a binary male/female distinction to be explored in the first place. How, then, do we avoid making this methodological error, given that two is generally thought to be the right number of genders?

Anne Grethe Solburg has also been looking at the differences between women and men in leadership roles. She concludes that the differences are only marginal. To all intents and purposes, male and female leaders are the same. And a masculine style of leadership does not predominate – not even among men.

Solburg's research uses four categories of leadership style, called the Bem Sex Role Inventory (BSRI). The styles are masculine, feminine, androgynous and undifferentiated. She found that as many men used a feminine leadership style as women used a masculine leadership style. The masculine style – which, remember, includes both men and women leaders – was used by only 30% of the sample.

Those using an androgynous style – that is, both masculine and feminine – were in the minority at 22% of the sample, but they reported having the best innovation climate in their groups. The population using the androgynous style was split equally between women and men.

Androgyny seems to go along with the qualities supposedly valued in contemporary leadership: openness, a coaching style and orientation towards change. But Solberg's results also challenge the notion that gender diversity in organisations leads to greater efficiency, creativity and profitability, one of the main arguments on which Norway's well-known gender quota for public company boards is based. "Diversity and efficiency doesn't happen just because a board or a group is comprised of both women and men," states Solberg. "In order to benefit from the alleged gender differences, we need to develop a new type of culture of communication that is inclusive for heterogeneous groups, that takes into account that people are different – regardless of biological gender. You have to cultivate the difference."[26]

Difference matters, but gender isn't the source of difference. People are.

And as for neuroscience.....

The same point applies to neuroscience research. The last twenty years or so have seen enormous advances in neuroscience and the biosciences. Many of the discoveries made in these fields serve to undermine earlier over-neat assumptions about the organisation of the brain, its development and the role of the environment in shaping how our minds work.

Neuroscientists have discovered that far from being "hardwired" at birth – or, indeed, at any set stage of development – the brain is plastic. That is, it can and does change in structure and function. For example, an area of the brain responsible for dealing with spatial information is larger in London taxi drivers than in other people. The taxi drivers didn't start out that way; doing "the knowledge", the in-depth test of routes and places of interest in London that all London taxi drivers have to pass in order to work, stimulated growth in their knowledge equipment. It makes no sense to talk about *the* human brain, let alone the male brain or the female brain. Brains keep changing and the focus on brain studies today is overwhelmingly on plasticity, rather than "hardwiring".

Meanwhile, bioscientists studying how the genome governs development have found that while DNA may indeed be a code, nature does not simply "read off" the code like a computer program. The new field of epigenetics studies the myriad other mechanisms that contribute to cellular and structural development, in particular the substances and circumstances that activate or suppress the expression of genes. The environment of a developing person is a crucial part of the story – not just a setting, but an active participant in the shaping of the organism.

One popular theory about male and female brains is Simon Baron Cohen's. In his book, *The Essential Difference*, he writes: "The female brain is predominantly hardwired for empathy. The male brain is predominantly hardwired for understanding and building systems."[27] Even though he is careful not to state that men and women are completely different, this conclusion ignores the fact that empathy has been demonstrated to depend on social situations and cultural expectations as much as on motivation and ability.

The research has been criticised on many counts, but his conclusions are now popularly accepted as fact. As the neuroscientist Cordelia Fine says: "There is something shocking about the discrepancy between the weakness of the scientific data on the one hand and the strength of the popular claims on the other."[28]

To make matters worse – or more interesting – the disruption to earlier theories comes from two directions. Taking the idea of brain functions first, it's not just that the whereabouts of a particular function are becoming uncertain, but that the notion of coherent, stable functions is also becoming less intelligible. For example, we aren't just asking, "Where does memory live in the brain?" – we're also asking, "What *is* memory, anyway?" Similarly, in genetics-with-epigenetics we can ask both, "Why can't we find a gene for optimism?" and, "Is there really such a thing as optimism?" (To be clear, of course we remember things, but this does not mean that memories are necessarily things. We can be optimistic, but this doesn't mean there is such a thing as an optimistic personality.) In other words, the research is complex, confusing and contradicts our preconceived ideas.

The hardwired, fixed-brain model fits better with our stereotypes about people. However, the message is beginning to get through. Writing for a business audience, entrepreneur Naveen Jain puts it like this:

> The simple truth is, if men are from Mars, then so are women. Any difference in gender is more a product of nurture than anything genetic or hardwired in our brains.

One of the widespread gender stereotypes states that women are "more emotional" than men. Until recently, it was widely assumed that our emotions were controlled by the limbic system of our brains. However, it turns out that these initial scientists were only partially right. We have learned that the prefrontal cortex plays an even greater role in our emotions and behaviour. Interestingly, there is no difference in the prefrontal cortex between men and women, and this part of the brain is not even fully developed until we are in our twenties.[29]

Reviewing recent studies, Jain concludes that "gender stereotypes are simply the confabulation of our own mind". Research into male and female brains is nothing new; Victorian scientists discovered that women's brains were smaller than men's brains, apparently failing to notice that men are generally bigger than women. When you make the mathematical correction, women's brains tend to be larger than men's.[30]

The long-standing beliefs about right-brain and left-brain specialisation are often cited to account for inherent differences between male and female thinking.[30] But "no one has yet demonstrated that female brains have more highly developed left hemispheres than do male brains or that male brains have more highly developed right hemispheres than do female brains".[31] In fact the right-brain/left-brain concept is recognised as a myth;[31] the assumed rigid specialisation of the hemispheres does not appear to exist. So the belief that a brain – or a half-brain – can be either female or male is specious.

Harris also argues persuasively that physiological differences linked to sex, however minor, can be amplified by cultural selection to produce greater apparent differences between the sexes. Such minor differences can also be suppressed by cultural pressures. Women, for instance, seem to have a better sense of taste than men, yet chefs are typically male, while women do the cooking at home – where Michelin stars don't count.

As an anthropologist, Harris is concerned with separating fact from myth. He is careful to apply this principle evenly: "I fear that I may be creating the impression that biological differences between the sexes are irrelevant, whereas it is merely the hypothetical and speculative status of some of the alleged differences to which I object".[30] This is a sentiment that gender commentators should take to heart. We need to be objective if we're to change the way things are at work and in the wider world.

The race to map the brain in terms of functions mirrors the race to crack the code of DNA. It turns out that each project is something of an illusion – or, at best, only a small part of a larger story. The idea that we can know what each part of the brain is "for" begins to look as misguided as the idea that there are genes "for" personality or behaviour traits.

The impact on leadership

One reason put forward for why women are disliked when they occupy leadership positions is that such women confound the expectation that only men occupy powerful roles. Female leaders break the tacit rule that leaders are always men.[6] Another reason may be their being seen as "threatening intruders".[32]

The traits women display when leading have been shown to impact how effective they are in leadership roles. Women who appear to be behaving like men can suffer from the backlash effect, as discussed in Chapter 6 – a series of social, economic or organisational punishments for acting against prescriptive stereotypes. However, research suggests that women can avoid the backlash effect by self-monitoring.[33] By choosing when and how to use more stereotypically masculine traits, women may be able to avoid being perceived as transgressing unwritten gender rules. Self-monitoring enables women to extend the range of styles they use according to the context, rather than electing to use more masculine traits as default behaviour. It's interesting that flexibility across the gender divide can be seen as key to women's progression, when flexibility itself is a female trait. This strategy of "impression management"[34] reminds us that advancement at work is not all about concrete results.

Eagly, Kakhijani and Klonsky[32] found that the style of leadership a woman adopted affected how she was evaluated. When adopting a more autocratic style of leadership, thereby displaying traits associated with the male stereotype, she was evaluated more negatively than when she adopted a democratic leadership style which contained more female-related traits. This suggests that it is not being a leader *per se* that leads to harsher evaluations of women, but rather the violation of social norms of expected behaviour.

This suggests that one way for a woman to be successful and not hinder her progression is to behave in a way congruent with gender stereotypes when in leadership positions, adopting styles that are more transformational. The problem with this approach is that it reaffirms both descriptive and prescriptive gender stereotypes.

Researchers Ginka Toegel and Jean-Louis Barsoux at IMD Business School in Switzerland found the same results in their research; that certain ways of behaving are more acceptable in men than women.[35] They identify both communal and agentic behaviours, while helpfully avoiding describing them as male and female. Table 5.2 lists examples of agentic and communal behaviour. However, they advise women to avoid being too agentic and too communal: the latter will draw attention to their femininity and the former will carry penalties for contravening the female stereotype. We understand why they would reach this conclusion, but they also make the point that leaders have to be authentic and that involves being yourself, at least in part. Self-regulation of behaviour is indeed an important indicator of potential, so being aware of your impact is no bad thing. But why is it more important for women than men?

Although men and women equally endorse descriptive gender stereotypes both implicitly and explicitly, there are gender differences in the sanction of prescriptive stereotypes. Women are less likely to endorse prescriptive stereotypes as explicitly as men, but they endorse them equally at the implicit level. This is probably why women experience more conflict – implicit and explicit beliefs are at odds with each other.

Rosabeth Moss Kanter[36] suggested that being in a minority in organisations brings its own special pressures. Women leaders, she said, will be categorised into one of four stereotypes or role traps:

Table 5.2: Avoiding the extremes.

Highly communal	Moderately communal	Neutral	Moderately agentic	Highly agentic
Giggling Putting welfare of others above own Gossiping Speaking softly Family enquiries	Smiling Nodding Open-handed gestures Recognition Sharing credit Active listening Responsiveness Thanking people publicly Speaking out against injustice Asking for or offering help Showing concern	Participating in work discussions Providing, seeking or summarising information Composed demeanour Self-deprecating humour Level voice Listening calmly	Gesticulating Sitting at the head of the table Standing when others sit Holding someone's gaze Low-pitched voice Shrugging Shaking head Sighing Slow vocal cadence Speaking up first	Pointing Table tapping Staring Husky voice Talking sports Sarcasm Yelling/raising voice Public putdown Swearing

- Mother: will be seen as warm, caring, unthreatening

- Iron maiden: will be seen as aggressive, tough, a bitch

- Seductress: will be seen as using her feminine wiles to influence and succeed

- Pet: will be seen as cute, adorable, funny.

This grouping was produced over thirty years ago, but more recent research by Judith Baxter shows that these archetypes, albeit in a modified form, are still with us. One impact is that it affects the way women in leadership positions speak.[37] Baxter, a professor of applied linguistics, has examined in depth the speech patterns of men and women in leadership positions, and has concluded that being aware of how they may be judged has an impact on their speech. Women use double-voiced discourse more than men – it is a way of second-guessing others or indirectly expressing an opinion by referencing someone else, for example. This approach was used in creative and flexible ways by women so that they had the greatest impact. Nevertheless, we need to understand that the difference in the use of language is not because of any biological or genetic reason; it is due to the position that many women leaders find themselves in.

Differences in motivation

The SHL research quoted earlier which found no gender differences in leadership style or potential did find differences in motivation to succeed to the most senior roles. The researchers divided motivational characteristics into "What gets me out of bed in the morning?" and "What brings me back the next day?" On the first criterion, men were motivated by the dimension "Power'" (taking responsibility, exercising authority and influencing others) and women by "Ease and security". On the second criterion women were motivated by "Recognition" and men by "Fear of failure". The authors were well aware of how such information can be taken out of context, and were careful to stress individual differences: "Not all men and all women are motivated to succeed in the same way." This finding has been echoed elsewhere, with women sometimes not wanting to take the most senior posts in an organisation, choosing other roles instead and sometimes leaving the organisation altogether.[38]

Women and men may view the goals of the corporation differently too. Research in Norway[21] found that boards with a higher representation of women on them were less likely to make people redundant at the start of a recession. But, again, research around this shows the difference to be small and, as always, we need to remember that women and men differ as individuals too.

As ever, there could be an alternative explanation for this. We were asked to review the gender diversity policy of a major British civil service department. The department had a target for women in senior positions of 40% by a particular deadline. With a year to go, the percentage of women in top roles was 38%, so there was nothing to worry about then. We talked to many people at different managerial levels and found that despite being in, Moss Kanter's terms, a balanced group, the women were still being treated as an outgroup. They were not involved in many of the key decisions and felt, at the most senior levels, like tokens. The experiences of the senior women were known to women at the grades below, and many told us that they were not prepared to take on the responsibilities in that sort of environment. This is not to say that differences in motivation don't exist, but the reasons for them have not been adequately explored yet.

Resetting our assumptions

The popular view that men and women are utterly and irreconcilably different is a myth. If we accept that men and women are indeed different then we should be embracing this wholeheartedly. Simon Baron Cohen, Steven Pinker and Nigel Nicholson, among others, embrace this view and ask us to accept it too. But embracing it means more than attending a workshop on "difference". It means that we actively channel men and women into different occupational domains. It means that we accept that most, if not all, of the high-status roles will be given to men. While many people are prepared to accept the argument that men and women are fundamentally different, they are not prepared to accept the full extent of the consequences.

Women and men are in fact remarkably similar, as we have seen in this chapter, and this simple fact applies to leadership as it does to most other areas of work. Seeing difference is not the same as being different. The research that reveals the biggest differences is based on 360-degree feedback data and interviews. For the former type of research, our stereotypes will impact on how we see the other person performing. Interview research suffers from framing bias: asking "What do you bring to leadership as a woman?" is not the same as asking "What do you bring as a leader?"

More in-depth studies, typically carried out by universities, show very little, if any, differences in leadership styles and effectiveness between men and women.

Many leading academic psychologists now conclude that we are on safer intellectual ground by saying there are no differences. Personality questionnaire data shows much the same outcome. But motivation to fill a senior role may differ overall between the genders. Is this a true difference, or is it a result of being in an outgroup, with the extra work that needs to be applied before one is noticed, recognised and valued?

Throughout history we have seen how men have taken higher-paid, higher-status jobs. Where women were allowed in, they were viewed as poachers, regarded as somehow illegitimate. Perhaps we should expect there to be resistance to women in leadership as it is directly related to power and influence. This dominance is not to be given up lightly. Women are now in leadership positions but the progress from being a token to a more balanced state is slow to non-existent. Indeed, we would suggest that *some* women have to succeed in order for the system to be maintained.

In continuing to privilege "male" styles of leadership over "female" ones, people are effectively denying the rationale for leadership. If leadership is about results, or direction, or togetherness, then what does it matter which (legal and ethical) leadership styles are used? The desire to prove that men and women are different in the way they lead fits in with Moss Kanter's observation that when women are in a minority, or are tokens, the dominant group will seek to accentuate differences as a means of ensuring that the other group is not seen as equal. This approach, sometimes referred to as gender essentialism, provides managers and leaders with a convenient get-out clause for not taking diversity more seriously. Managers who accept the gender essentialism approach are more likely to believe that the organisation's systems are fair and also that diversity strategies are discriminatory. Where this mindset prevails, managers are less likely to take action on diversity.[39]

Distinguishing between male and female styles is a way of preferring men over women, not a way of improving leadership performance or outcomes. It also provides a handy argument and rationale for those people not wishing to provide genuine equality.

A lot of time and effort has gone into trying to explain why men and women are so different. Time and again, in the work context, this is simply not proven. As Cordelia Fine says: "Pick a gender difference, any difference. Now watch very closely as – *poof!* – it's gone."[28]

References

1. Available at: http://www.leadernetwork.org/leaderdef.htm. Accessed 20 October 2013.

2. Prinz JJ. *Furnishing the Mind*. MIT Press; 2004.

3. Glick P, Fiske ST. 'The ambivalent sexism inventory: Differentiating hostile and benevolent sexism.' *Journal of Personality and Social Psychology* 1996; 70(3): 491–512.

4. Swim JK, Aikin KJ, Hall WS, Hunter BA. 'Sexism and racism: Old-fashioned and modern prejudices.' *Journal of Personality and Social Psychology* 1995; 68(2): 199.

5. Williams JE, Best DL. *Measuring Sex Stereotypes*. Sage Publications; 1990.

6. Rudman LA, Kilianski SE. 'Implicit and explicit attitudes toward female authority.' *Personality and Social Psychology Bulletin* 2000; 26(11): 1315–1328. doi:10.1177/0146167200263001.

7. Lord RG, Foti RJ, DeVader CL. 'A test of leadership categorization theory: Internal structure, information processing, and leadership perceptions.' *Organizational Behavior and Human Performance* 1984; 34: 343–378.

8. Offermann LR, Kennedy JK, Wirtz PW. 'Implicit leadership theories: Content, structure, and generalizability.' *The Leadership Quarterly* 1994; 5(1): 43–58.

9. Lyness KS, Heilman ME. 'When fit is fundamental: Performance evaluations and promotions of upper-level female and male managers.' *Journal of Applied Psychology* 2006; 91(4): 777–785. doi:10.1037/0021-9010.91.4.777.

10. Eagly AH, Karau SJ. 'Role congruity theory of prejudice toward female leaders.' *Psychological Review* 2002; 109(3): 573–598. doi:10.1037//0033-295X.109.3.573.

11. Heilman ME, Alcott VB. 'What I think you think of me: Women's reactions to being viewed as beneficiaries of preferential selection.' *Journal of Applied Psychology* 2001; 86 (4): 574. doi:10.1037//0021.

12. Heilman ME. 'Sex bias in work settings: The lack of fit model.' *Research in Organizational Behavior* 1983; 5: 269–298.

13. Powell GN. 'Gender and managerial stereotypes: Have the times changed?' *Journal of Management* 2002; 28(2): 177–193. doi:10.1177/014920630202800203.

14. Willemsen TM. 'Gender typing of the successful manager: A stereotype reconsidered.' *Sex Roles* 2002; 46: 385–391.

15. Eagly AH, Johannesen-Schmidt MC. 'The leadership styles of women and men.' *Journal of Social Issues* 2001; 57(4): 781–797.

16. Eagly AH, Karau SJ, Makhijani MG. 'Gender and the effectiveness of leaders: A meta-analysis.' *Psychological Bulletin* 1995; 117(1): 125–145.

17. Available at: www.apa.org/research/action/boss.aspx. Accessed 23 September 2013.

18. Robbins SP, Judge TA, Campbell TT. *Organizational Behaviour*. Pearson; 2010.

19. Landy FJ, Conte JM. *Work in the 21st Century*. John Wiley & Sons; 2009.

20. Woods SA, West MA. *The Psychology of Work and Organizations.* Cengage Learning/ EMEA; 2010.

21. Available at: http://dop.bps.org.uk/dop/women-at-the-top$.cfm. Accessed 24 September 2013.

22. SHL Talent Report 2012 Provides Unprecedented Insight on the Global Workforce | News | Company | SHL US. Available at: http://www.deltaknot.com/download/SHL-Talent-Report-USE.pdf . Accessed 20 October 2013.

23. Available at: http://blog.talentinnovations.com/2012/10/17/new-study-highlights-the-differences-between-male-and-female-leaders/. Accessed 20 October 2013.

24. Kahneman D. *Thinking, Fast and Slow.* Penguin; 2012.

25. Available at: http://www.iddas.com/Research/charts/Board%20Dynamics-a%20female%20perspective-Executive%20Summary.pdf. Accessed 20 October 2013.

26. Available at: http://euroscientist.com/2013/04/gender-differences-in-leadership-are-a-myth/. Accessed 24 September 2013.

27. Baron-Cohen S. *The Essential Difference: Male and Female Brains and the Truth about Autism.* ReadHowYouWant; 2010.

28. Fine C. *Delusions of Gender.* Icon Books; 2011.

29. Available at: http://www.inc.com/naveen-jain/study-men-and-women-do-think-the-same.html. Accessed 24 September 2013.

30. Harris M. *Our Kind.* Harper Perennial; 1990.

31. Available at: http://www.psychologytoday.com/blog/brain-myths/201206/why-the-left-brain-right-brain-myth-will-probably-never-die. Accessed 24 September 2013.

32. Eagly AH, Makhijani MG, Klonsky BG. 'Gender and the evaluation of leaders: A meta-analysis.' *Psychological Bulletin* 1992; 111(1): 3–22. doi:10.1037/0033-2909.111.1.3.

33. O'Neill OA, O'Reilly CA III. 'Reducing the backlash effect: Self-monitoring and women's promotions.' *Journal of Occupational and Organizational Psychology* 2011; 84(4): 825–832. doi:10.1111/j.2044-8325.2010.02008.x.

34. Rudman LA, Phelan JE. 'Backlash effects for disconfirming gender stereotypes in organizations.' *Research in Organizational Behavior* 2008; 28: 61–79. doi:10.1016/j.riob.2008.04.003.

35. Available at: http://www.europeanbusinessreview.com/?p=6785. Accessed 20 October 2013.

36. Kanter RM. *Men and Women of the Corporation.* PublicAffairs; 2008.

37. Baxter J. *The Language of Female Leadership.* Palgrave Macmillan; 2010.

38. Pinker S. *The Sexual Paradox.* Simon & Schuster; 2008.

39. Available at: http://www.mbs.edu/facultyresearch/ethicalleadership/Documents/Centre%20for%20Ethical%20Leadership%20-%20Targets%20and%20Quotas.pdf. Accessed 20 October 2013.

6

GENDERWATCH: RECOGNISING GENDER BIAS AND ITS EFFECTS AT WORK

"The greatest trick the Devil ever pulled was convincing the world he didn't exist." (Roger "Verbal" Kint in *The Usual Suspects*)

At the heart of this book is the impact of gender stereotypes. Stereotypes can show themselves in many forms and so we need to be aware of them and how they appear in organisations. There are those who think that we are so modern in our thinking, so aware and enlightened, that stereotyping can't be a prevalent issue in our society and our workplaces. Yet you only have to look at the movement towards valuing the differences between men and women to see that the stereotypes of old have simply mutated rather than disappeared. Now, rather than sounding critical and negative, we appreciate that men and women have fundamentally different qualities and characters, and believe that by recognising difference we can create more effective workplaces. This view, if allowed to take hold, is dangerous precisely because it is readily accepted. And it is more likely to be accepted because it is positive.

The approach of valuing difference is presented as profound, progressive and positive. It is anything but. It is a reinterpretation of age-old views about men and women dressed up in New Age language. Instead of addressing the popular myths about men and women, it accepts them as fact and delivers them repackaged to organisations in such a way that we don't have to change our attitudes – our attitudes were correct in the first place.

In this chapter we summarise key gender biases, when they are more likely to be applied and how they manifest themselves in a number of work domains.

This chapter is not intended to be a template or a model, nor a set of plans or priorities, nor a strategy or a scheme. It is, however, intended to provoke a different way of viewing the world, to question aspects of work and the workplace that we have taken for granted. We hope that this will help people to challenge assumptions that usually remain untested and to discuss topics that will otherwise continue to be avoided.

Table 6.1: Summary of key biases.

Type of bias	Description	Manifestation
Descriptive stereotypes	• Beliefs about how men and women differ (e.g. men are agentic/competent, women are communal/warm) • Established at an early age, differences are seen as natural and lasting	• Focus on behaviours that confirm the stereotype and ignore contradictory information • Interpret behaviour in line with our stereotypical beliefs, e.g. the man contributed more to the meeting, or the woman spoke too much • Attribute success and failure to different factors for men and women, e.g. external factors contribute to a woman's success (luck, an easy client, a good team); internal factors to a male's (e.g. skill, perseverance) • Women in non-stereotypical roles need to provide greater evidence of high performance than males for employment rewards

Type of bias	Description	Manifestation
		• Assumptions about which roles, jobs, projects and overseas assignments women will and will not be interested in
Use of positive stereotypes	• Use of complimentary terms to describe women on stereotypical feminine traits • Shows up in the "men and women are different and complementary" approach • Leads to reinforcement of the status quo	• Described as a need to value the difference that men and women bring • Emphasise the differences and ignore data showing women and men do not differ in competences or style of working • Women and men both agree on the stereotypes, so little challenge when described in these terms • Endorsed by leaders and other influential people
Innuendo effect	• Where some traits are referred to, no matter how positively, our attention is drawn to those qualities not mentioned. We assume that qualities not mentioned are not present. (This is a direct consequence of the "valuing men and women's differences" approach.)	• Describe a woman as possessing stereotypical feminine traits but omit information on other aspects of her competence
Being a parent	• The perceived role of each parent is different: Dad is the breadwinner and Mum the carer and homemaker. Their mutual dependence makes these views very difficult to change	• When a man becomes a father it typically has a positive effect. They maintain perceptions of competence and gain perceptions of warmth

Type of bias	Description	Manifestation
Being a parent	• The expectations and the associated stereotypes for mothers and fathers have an impact on perceptions of men and women at work	• When a woman becomes a mother her perceived competence is reduced • A mother's commitment to her job will be questioned and her primary interests will be seen to lie elsewhere • Assumptions made about her commitment to work • Assumptions also made about the father's role within the family
Stereotype threat	• The feeling, in certain relevant situations, that a person has when they fear that they may confirm the negative stereotype that is associated with their group	• Performance is reduced in a context where people are aware of the stereotypes associated with their perceived group • This awareness of the stereotype leads to a greater probability of failing in a task or doing less well • Fewer women apply for leadership roles because of this • It is the behaviour of others in the situation that brings on the condition. They are contributing to the under-performance
Ingroups and outgroups	• Ingroups and outgroups are formed based on gender	• Informal networks create a sense of support for those involved

Type of bias	Description	Manifestation
Ingroups and outgroups	• Strong informal networks are formed not explicitly based on gender but they may nevertheless exclude women	• Networking helps in career progression • Greater access to information and resources leads to enhanced performance • The ingroup will have greater out-of-hours socialisation, which helps to maintain and strengthen the bonds between the group members • Failure to invite outgroup members to social events • The events themselves are designed to reflect the interests of the ingroup and be of less interest to the outgroup • Views of the outgroup will not be listened to; e.g. when a woman criticises the behaviour of her male colleagues, she is more likely to be ignored if she is seen as an outgroup member • Ingroup refuses to change when criticised by an outgroup member. The criticism is seen as a challenge to their self-esteem and they will try to ignore, minimise or even ridicule the observations • Leads to higher turnover among female team members

Type of bias	Description	Manifestation
Prescriptive stereotypes	<ul><li>Beliefs about how men and women *should* behave</li><li>Aim is to maintain the status quo and dependency between men and women: men are dependent on women to look after the home and care for family so they can have their role as breadwinner; women are dependent on men to provide for the household</li><li>Creates a double bind for ambitious women because to be successful they need to behave in ways that violate the prescriptions</li></ul>	<ul><li>Penalties are applied to those who violate prescribed ways of behaving</li><li>Women are penalised more than men for not behaving in expected ways</li><li>Men are able to be more aggressive at work because it is more expected of them. A woman *should not* be aggressive so is penalised for the same behaviour</li><li>Women *should* be caring, kind and good listeners. If they do not show this behaviour, they are penalised</li><li>When a woman violates the stereotype, she is less liked and less influential. At work this will make her less effective</li><li>As a consequence both men and women will be cautious about breaking away from the prescribed ways of behaving. Behaving according to prescribed norms further reinforces the view that men and women are different</li></ul>
Hostile sexism	<ul><li>A fundamental belief in the "natural order" of the world</li></ul>	<ul><li>Negative views about whether women are able to perform well in non-stereotypical roles</li></ul>

Type of bias	Description	Manifestation
Hostile sexism	• Responding negatively to someone in a non-stereotypical role	• Women may be viewed positively on work-related dimensions but seen negatively on personal traits (e.g. selfish, greedy, cold, aggressive) • Overt behaviour, such as the use of sexist language and jokes • Unwilling to review or change negative opinion of women in the light of contradictory information
Benevolent sexism	• Less overt and obvious form of sexism • View women in stereotypical or restricted roles positively	• Behaviour permitted depends on context, e.g. assertiveness appreciated in a PA but penalised in a female leader • Rewards women who stay in traditional roles, penalises those who do not • Can be displayed by women as well as men • Uncertainty as to whether one has experienced benevolent sexism leads to an internal focus (self-questioning) and diminished performance

Type of bias	Description	Manifestation
Ambivalent sexism	• A combination of both hostile and benevolent sexism • Sexist behaviour towards women has less of an impact when it occurs in roles that women typically perform well • Sexist behaviour towards women has much more impact in jobs that men excel in	• Men, in particular, display positive behaviours towards women in traditional roles and negative behaviours to those in non-traditional roles • May find expression in appraisal systems where women may receive praise for their work but not the commensurate pay award • May find expression in promotion situations where women will be considered as high performers but with less potential than equivalent men • Women may be accepted into non-stereotypical roles in an acting or stand-in capacity only, while a more suitable candidate is found

Gender bias is more likely to be applied in certain situations, and we describe these in the next section.

When is bias more likely to be applied?

Table 6.2: When gender bias is more likely to be applied.

When roles are gendered	• Jobs are gendered and, without our realising it, this fact alone can influence the decisions we make • When being considered for a role that is stereotypically performed by men, the bar will be higher for a woman and she will need to provide more evidence of competence than her male counterparts • When women apply for jobs typically done by a woman, implicitly the bar will be lower for her than for a man. This also happens when a man applies for a job typically done by a man
Few women in a role, unit or department	• The fewer women there are in work units, the more salient their gender becomes. This influences our expectations and, in turn, our evaluations of them • Their visibility will mean that their performance will come under greater scrutiny than men's • As members of the outgroup their faults will be highlighted more than those of men • They will be viewed as tokens • They will have less access to networks
When femininity is salient	• Factors that make gender more salient, such as physical attractiveness[1] or being a mother,[2] increase the likelihood of stereotypes and – consequently – bias
Ambiguity over...	• Role requirements and the use of subjective terms such as "charismatic" or "resilient" • How to combine performance criteria to come up with an overall rating • Who is responsible for success – in these situations, we are more likely to attribute success to men
When the task has a diversity objective attached to it	• Women in an outgroup are likely to be evaluated more negatively than men when there is a diversity goal attached to a task or initiative. So mentioning that the group was compiled to ensure it has a diverse representation is likely[3] to lead to the belief that women are there "to bring diversity", not because they are the most competent person for the job

Time pressure	• We are more likely to make biased decisions when we are under pressure • Limited time availability means that we are more likely to make more conservative decisions, less likely to consider different options and less likely to challenge decisions that are taken • In such scenarios, less time is taken to evaluate the evidence for each person against specific criteria. We are more likely to draw on overall impressions including personal "fit" and potential. While these qualities can be rationalised as being critical for anyone in any role, they are typically very subjectively assessed and allow bias into the process
High cognitive load	• Being distracted, not concentrating on the task in hand, and thinking about other things are other ways of considering this factor • We can only give 100% of attention to anything, so if we are thinking of other things then our focus is divided • If we are making calls, writing emails, etc. when decisions are being made then there will be an increased likelihood that stereotypes and unconscious associations will intrude into our decision-making process

Bias and its application at work

The following section summarises how bias can manifest itself in three key work domains – teamworking, leadership and flexible working – and the impact it has as a consequence.

Teamworking

Much of the work we carry out is group- or team-based. It should not be surprising that our views about gender are manifested in team and group behaviour. Women in women-only teams and men in men-only teams behave in the same way. But mix the genders up and we see very different patterns of behaviour emerging. Women's behaviour in the two environments varies more than men's, which clearly indicates that the context of the team has an influence.

The leader's behaviour is important. If the leader creates an ingroup and an outgroup then they will behave differently towards each member of the team, depending on how close they feel to them. The gendered nature of team activities can be seen through people's conversations and how inclusive they are in networking activities, and formal and informal social events.

Table 6.3: Teamworking.

Behaviour in mixed teams	• Men tend to talk more • Men tend to use more visual signs of dominance and assertiveness (e.g. body language) • Women do better when the task is seen as stereotypically female. Men do better when the task is seen as stereotypically male • Men are more likely to be chosen for the high-status roles
Language in mixed teams	• When in mixed teams, women adopt different styles of language • Conversations in male-dominated teams and organisations revolve around male preoccupations and interests. Conversations may not be designed to exclude women in such teams but they have this effect • Women tend to be less assertive in mixed teams and display more signals of acquiescence • To be successful in mixed teams, women have to adopt styles of language that enable them to make their point but which also conform to expectations of how women should behave • Women adopt a style of language that is more considerate of others and could be described as more inclusive. Their language is more supportive than leading. Others in teams expect this of them
Leader behaviour	• Leaders will rarely initiate conversations with outgroup members • There will be little discussion about performance • Little help or support with difficult work, thus increasing the chance of failing or underperforming • Low quality of interaction with outgroup members. Relationships are focused on the task in hand; very little interest is shown in the person • Leader allows little flexibility about how the role is to be carried out. An outgroup member has little opportunity to negotiate the role and, consequently, the role will feel constrained and restricted

Leadership

The reason why there are so few women in leadership roles in so many of our organisations is not because of different styles, ambitions or talent. It is because we *expect* leaders to be men. This expectation drives a whole series of behaviours, from the way we develop leadership criteria to the way we view potential. Furthermore, while men can and do display a range of leadership styles, women are more effective when they adopt a transformational style. It may well be that women who are more autocratic and transactional are less likely than men to be considered as leaders and so are less likely to gain the most senior roles.

There are many more women in leadership positions in the third sector but, even though these leaders are managing huge resources with often very complex cultures, they are not seen as being on a par with "captains of industry". Private sector companies, with their executive search partners in tow, could find many highly talented women running large organisations – women who could easily act as non-executive directors if only recruiters would open their minds to the possibilities.

"Playing the game" in organisations – that is, being political – has long been recognised as a necessary, if perhaps undesirable, prerequisite for succeeding. Such behaviour includes promoting yourself and your achievements. Once again, though, we find prescriptive stereotypes exerting their influence. We expect men to self-promote and women to be more modest and humble – as if modesty and humility are in women's nature. The personality questionnaire data shows this is not the case. Instead we find that women are caught in a double bind: if they don't self-promote they are not visible enough to be considered for senior roles, but if they do they are penalised by some for being viewed as pushy and less likeable. In other words, they don't fit.

We can contribute to the success or failure of women in non-traditional roles, including leadership, by the attitudes we take towards them. Failing to recognise that it may be more difficult for a woman in these positions is not treating her equally; it is poor management. People have different needs and where a woman is in a minority it is the responsibility of the manager or leader to be aware of the additional pressures she may be under. The attitudes of team members also contribute to the individual's performance.

Table 6.4: Leadership.

Leadership prototypes	• Our expectations of who will be in a leadership position are influenced by the people we have seen occupying them • Leadership is seen, implicitly and sometimes explicitly, as being a male preserve • Men are preferred for high-status positions in organisations • Men are seen to "fit" better with such roles – a highly subjective judgement • The criteria developed for leadership roles are usually described in stereotypically male terms. This can prime assessors to prefer male candidates • Women as well as men have a bias towards men in leadership roles. Although it may be comforting to know that female and male colleagues agree on an assessment that the man was the best candidate, the assessment may not be fair
Performance versus potential	• Performance is typically more objective – based on historic data • However, performance for women is higher when they are in a female-typed role than a male-typed one • For more senior roles and for male-typed positions, women's success is more likely to be attributed to external factors (e.g. a good team or luck) and men's success is more likely to be attributed to internal factors (e.g. skill or vision) • These attributions can be critical when assessments are being made about someone's potential for leadership roles
Perceptions of leadership and status beliefs	• We have expectations about who should exercise authority – status beliefs • When these status beliefs are defied, there is a backlash which includes being seen as less trustworthy and consequently becoming less influential • Women are liked less in leadership positions because they breach people's expectations • They are also seen as cold, selfish and poor team-mates

Leadership style	• Women who adopt certain transformational leadership styles are viewed more positively than those who behave more transactionally
	• Where women behave autocratically they are viewed more harshly than autocratic men
	• Assertive women in leadership roles are viewed more harshly than assertive men and non-assertive women
	• Women behaving like this are seen as less competent
Double binds	• To be a leader, there is a need to self-promote
	• We expect men to behave in this way but not women
	• When women self-promote it is viewed more negatively, as it runs counter to our expectations
	• This leaves ambitious women in a double bind: if they don't self-promote they will not be recognised, but when they do they are criticised
Language	• Women's language is more tentative than men's when leading a team. This is seen as more influential for them

Flexible working

We also have an expectation about the way a job should be carried out. We are wary of people who adopt alternative working arrangements (the phrase itself hints at our suspicions) and see them as less trustworthy, less motivated and less reliable.

Table 6.5: Flexible working.

Working "normally"	• There is an expectation about how work should be done
	• The ideal is that it will be done between certain hours, at a particular location. This is especially true for managerial positions
	• Other arrangements are seen as deviant and so are not to be trusted
	• Time deviants, particularly part-time employees, are penalised for working in this fashion. They are less likely to be promoted, to be considered for other roles and to be appraised
	• This impacts on both genders but, since more women work flexibly, it will affect them more

Bias and its impact on key processes

In this section we look at the impact of gender bias on three key processes: recruitment and selection; performance management; and assessments of potential.

Table 6.6: Gender bias in key processes.

Recruitment and selection	• Criteria that are used. The language that is used for senior management jobs is highly gendered, using phrases that equate to stereotypically male attributes • Advertisements for these jobs will reflect the criteria, and consequently will appeal more to male than female applicants • References have been shown to be biased and will reflect the referee's own perceptions. Women are more likely to be described in communal terms and men in more agentic ones. This may be enough to get people shortlisted, but will create a pre-judgement in the minds of interviewers as to the suitability of the candidates • The gender of the people currently doing the role will influence who is seen as most suitable for it • Where someone behaves in a stereotype-inconsistent way, they will be less likely to be hired • Someone wishing to work flexibly will be viewed less favourably
Performance management	• Where women are in a minority their behaviour will be under greater scrutiny • This could lead to more negative evaluations • Where ambivalent sexism exists, women will be rewarded more when they are in roles consistent with their gender • Ambivalent sexism may lead to women receiving more praise but less money than their male counterparts • Part-time workers are less likely to receive an appraisal
Assessments of potential	• Attributions of success for women and men in management positions differ. Women's success is more likely to be attributed to some external factors, but men's will more likely be attributed to their skill or personality

Assessments of potential	• When being considered for a leadership role, more evidence will be sought for the suitability of female candidates
	• Role prototypes are male in orientation, leading to a bias, albeit unknowingly in some occasions, towards men
	• Leadership roles have a male association which needs to be acknowledged
	• Part-time and other forms of flexible working will be viewed with suspicion and candidates will be treated warily
	• Women behaving counter-stereotypically will experience a backlash. They will, unfairly, be less trusted and less liked, which are serious drawbacks when being considered for higher roles

Gender bias has an impact on judgements and decision-making in numerous ways. Being able to recognise the bias at play will enable prejudice against women in the workplace to at least be discussed and – hopefully – addressed. A particular concern we have is the use of positive stereotypes (with the related issue of the innuendo effect). They are pervasive and important to watch out for – both men and women fall into the trap of endorsing these biases. Women are not more communal than men, and men are not more agentic than women, nor should we expect them to be.

In this chapter, we have highlighted a number of ways in which bias can be seen at play in the workplace. In Chapter 7, we consider applications of bias in more detail, taking a key personnel process and exploring how and where bias may be present at each stage.

References

Heilman ME, Stopeck MH. 'Being attractive, advantage or disadvantage? Performance-based evaluations and recommended personnel actions as a function of appearance, sex, and job type.' *Organizational Behavior and Human Decision Processes* 1985; 35(2): 202–215.

Heilman ME, Okimoto TG. 'Motherhood: A potential source of bias in employment decisions.' *Journal of Applied Psychology* 2008; 93(1): 189–198. doi:10.1037/0021-9010.93.1.189.

Heilman ME, Welle B. 'Disadvantaged by diversity? The effects of diversity goals on competence perceptions.' *Journal of Applied Social Psychology* 2006; 36(5): 1291–1319.

7

TAKING ACTION AGAINST GENDER BIAS

Understanding gender bias, its origins, development, power and centrality in today's workplace – these are necessary preparatory steps for tackling the detrimental effects of gender bias that are holding our organisations back. But we also need to take action. Challenging bias is everybody's job, so we need to make it part of everything we do.

Here we apply the field guide presented in Chapter 6 to a sample business process: hiring and promotion. The aim is to show how gender bias operates in a real-world setting and to demonstrate the actions that can be taken to counteract it.

Hiring, reward and promotion systems are central to the procedures and habits that bias decisions towards men. But all an organisation's key processes must be audited thoroughly and regularly, with attention paid to practice as well as policy, beginning with the very way we conceive roles.

Selection criteria

The selection criteria we develop will guide who we look for and how we go about it. But such criteria can also prime us towards one gender or another.

Take this example from an organisation we worked with, a leading multinational in the energy sector. Their leadership development team were perplexed as to why so few women were in senior positions. We were shown their leadership criteria, which had been developed by psychologists. There were six components, three of which were Deploy, Engage and Execute. We couldn't help but be amused: they were essentially looking for a soldier. And, given that the stereotyped image of a soldier is male, they may as well have said that they were looking for a man. (Another criterion was that candidates needed Vision – and, as we have already seen, women can't possibly have that!)

This type of language, and the thinking it results from, seems to pervade many organisations and has been particularly noticeable since the start of the global recession. When times are tough, the tough get going; so businesses need leaders who are competitive, courageous and even combative. Leaders seem to be increasingly attracted to military-style criteria. Perhaps this is because they are fabricating not just a specification of what they are looking for but a description of how they see themselves. Business leaders may be decisive, even bold – but are they really courageous? No one risks life or limb by sitting in meetings or typing at a keyboard – and no workplace need be a battlefield. The psychologists who developed these warlike criteria must have been – consciously or unconsciously – indulging the egos of those paying the bills.

Criteria which pander to male stereotypes and the prototype of the male leader make gender salient and are biased towards men. And they are not even accurate or helpful. There are broad categories of leadership style: laissez-faire, transactional and transformational leadership. Laissez-faire leadership is a passive, do-nothing, "let's wait and see" approach. Transactional leadership is the prevailing type of leadership today: focus on the task, get things done and engage people enough to ensure efficiency – but no more. This is the legacy of the engineering approach to management. And it works.

Transformational leadership, on the other hand, involves and engages people in the tasks to be performed. It is a way of leading that succeeds in combining a results orientation with a concern for individuals and their motivation. This form of leadership has been described as having an androgynous style, meaning that it is neither stereotypically male nor female. It also has the great advantage of being the most effective at getting results.

Shifting to a transformational leadership style is a simple change anyone can make if they want to. However, it means that those of us involved in developing leadership criteria need to be strong enough to manage the egos of those in power and to resist their desire to see themselves tacitly represented as heroes.

Attracting applicants

Once we have our criteria sorted out we can look for suitable applicants. We may delegate the task to an executive search firm, or do it in-house. Sadly, both routes tend to produce bland, hackneyed and unrealistic messages to candidates. The prose seems to get worse as the pay on offer gets higher. Every organisation is exclusively interested in people with excellent skills, who have succeeded at the highest levels, and whose passion for achievement remains undimmed by a lifetime of perfect performance in the face of near-insurmountable odds... Ad copy like this is not only unhelpful (because it fails to say anything meaningful about the role in question); it will also appeal more to male candidates because it reinforces the male leadership prototype.

In a programme for the BBC about women in leadership, the authors were asked to write one recruitment advertisement that would appeal to women and one that would put them off. The off-putting one was easy to write – ridiculously easy. We simply copied and pasted some choice verbiage from ads we found online. The "good" ad took much more thought. For a start, we found precious little to model it on or inspire our efforts. Ultimately, our description of the job and its demands remained the same, but we described the organisational culture in a completely different way.

The "good" ad states clearly that the organisation actively seeks diversity and will support the successful candidate in their role. The two advertisements were shown to a group of women, all of whom preferred the "good" one. (One of the panel liked both.) So, apparently little things such as the wording of an ad can make a big difference. The wording designed to attract female candidates addressed concerns – possibly unconscious concerns – that women may have when considering senior roles. They may believe they are not *quite* ready for senior positions. If you show that you know how people may feel when stepping up to a senior role, then such concerns are decreased.

Advertisement 1—Chief Operating Officer

We have become one of the UK's fastest growing businesses by aggressively increasing our market share both here and internationally.

We are now seeking a new chief Operating Officer who can take our business to the next level of growth.

Reporting directly to the CEO, the role is a demanding one requiring relentless focus on achieving our ambitious strategic goals. We are looking for someone who is ambitious, driven, well networked and with a demonstrable successful track record working at this level. An outstanding leader, you'll have strong business acumen, with excellent strategic skills as well as the necessary gravitas to be able to influence and work with an equally ambitious and driven group of people.

This full-time role entails engaging with our customers, deploying our resources effectively and executing the strategic plan to deliver our growth plan over the next 5 years.

The demands are great but the rewards are also. The package is extremely competitive for the person who excels in this role.

If you are interested apply to.....

Advertisement 2—Chief Operating Officer

We are one of Britain's fastest growing businesses based on our philosophy of team work, excellence in customer service and the ability to deliver what we promise.

We are looking for a new Chief Operating Officer to join our successful executive team.

Reporting to the CEO, you'll be expected to make a significant contribution to our ambitious growth plans over the next five years.

We are looking for someone who understands modern-day markets and who appreciates the diversity of our customers and our staff.

You'll have a track record of success, both in terms of delivering strategic plans, of creating great teams and creating a culture of sustained success.

Difference and diversity is what has made us successful so we are looking for someone with different approaches and innovative ways of thinking and working. As a value driven business how you achieve results is as important as what you achieve

Your key responsibilities will be to turn our strategic plans into actions and to deliver results. To do this you'll need to be a good communicator, be able to engage and empathise with people at all levels in the organisations and understand our customers' needs.

If you are interested apply to.....

References and soundings

References may be sought during a selection process. For promotion processes, co-workers may be asked for their views of the candidate. In both cases, be aware of how male and female candidates are being described. Gender stereotyping may occur here with men being described in more agentic ways and women in more communal ways. As we have seen, the way in which people see themselves and how others see them differ. This is why there are differences between personality questionnaire data and 360-degree feedback reports. It is almost as if we are using two subtly different dictionaries to describe each gender.

Even if the stereotyped descriptions are framed very positively for women, the innuendo effect will make us aware of the missing qualities, and these are typically the ones that display greater agency or the ability to get things done. To overcome this tendency, we need to:[1]

- Provide information on each individual's unique contribution
- Verify that women had a role in the success
- Provide clear evidence that the woman has succeeded previously in male-typed roles.

Since an unmentioned dimension has a powerful effect on our judgement, it is important that we include both dimensions in every evaluative description we make of an individual. If we don't, an unspoken "but..." will undermine the rationality of the decision-making process, allowing bias to distort our actions. If one dimension is omitted from a description, then we assume the individual lacks that dimension – and the competences that go with it.

Attributing success

Success is success. What could be simpler? Unfortunately, identifying and valuing success is not straightforward. Although everyone may agree on the outcomes, we may not agree on how they were achieved.

In one promotion panel that we were asked to observe, a female candidate was being discussed. The sponsoring manager said, "She is leading a great team." One of his colleagues responded: "Ah, does she lead the team or does the team lead her?" This somewhat gnomic comment identified the reason for success, which lay not within the candidate herself but in her good fortune in having not just a talented team but a self-organising one too. This type of attribution means that women are less likely to be seen as the architects of their success, particularly in non-stereotypical roles, and more seen as the beneficiaries of a benevolent fortune. Be wary of such descriptions. In this instance the sponsoring manager replied: "What are you talking about? And when have we ever said this about any of the men we are discussing?"

The sponsor's challenge was enough to draw attention to the cryptic nature of the comment and to focus attention on the facts. The candidate was, in this case, promoted. Being aware is one thing, but being prepared to stand up and challenge colleagues is another.

Where attributing success is difficult, perhaps because of the complex nature of the task or interdependencies among groups, women in non-stereotypical roles will be assessed more negatively. This also links to the double bind that women face when self-promoting. While we expect people who wish to get on to self-promote, we prefer it when men do it and penalise women when they do. Hence the more guarded, modest statements that women are more likely to make when describing their successes. This is not because women are naturally more self-deprecating – it is because of the way we expect them to behave.

Creating shortlists and pipelines

When an organisation begins to pay attention to issues of gender bias and makes managers more accountable for their decisions, more women will be added to shortlists and the talent pipeline. This is obviously a good thing because, as the saying goes, you have to be in it to win it. But it is invariably the case that women will not progress much further. There are a number of reasons for this.

First, because managers may feel they have been forced to put women forward, they may view women less favourably. Second, research has shown that in non-critical situations women and minorities will be praised and welcomed but will be omitted when the key decision has to be made. This is an example of ambivalent sexism in operation. The reward – that appointment, that promotion – remains, tantalisingly, just out of reach.

We met a female manager in Belgium who was on the company's talent pipeline. She had been told she would be ready for promotion in the next two to three years. And she had been told so for the last twelve years.

Making the final decision and onboarding

All of the biases discussed above can play a part in the final decision, along with several others. In an organisation we worked with recently, we found that in the round-table discussions to decide who should be promoted, there was a preference for candidates whom all the panellists knew. Those individuals who were better networked were better known. Now, being part of a network is related to whether or not you are in the ingroup. As we have seen, more senior positions virtually require people who are in the network. Being a member of the outgroup means not finding out about opportunities as well as not being visible to the key influencers. We asked the senior executives in this company to examine and extend their networks to ensure that some of the female high potentials were included.

Action on ingroups needs to be extended to all teams. Are there some people who we value more than others? Some who we involve more? Some whose opinion we value more? These are highly important questions. It is our daily interactions that determine how included, challenged and supported we feel. In turn, these effects have a bearing on whether we will stay with an organisation or not.

How would we feel if a candidate for a management position wanted to work from home? Or, worse, work part-time? This option is, even with all advantages technology affords us, seen as time deviancy. We can do something very simple to help counter this effect: we can reframe the question. Rather than asking,

"How can this be done?" we can instead say, "What could we do to make this work?" This straightforward action will lead to more creative thinking rather than closing the discussion down. Also, be aware of prescriptive stereotypes coming into play if a man makes such a request. He may be penalised for not conforming to the male prescribed role.

Finally, don't treat this as a numbers game. Publications like the Davies Report make the changing of numbers their priority. But you can be sure of this: set a target for boards to be 25% female and 25% will be achieved. One owner of a headhunting business told us recently that boards are definitely more interested in female candidates now, and placing the first and sometimes the second woman is becoming easier. After that, though, interest and motivation decline as they have achieved what they set out to do. This is not a judgement on the female applicants, but an insight into the attitudes of the male majority. They have done *just* enough to satisfy onlookers and that is as far as they need or want to go.

Remember this: in order for the status quo to remain a few women *must* – and we are choosing our words carefully here – be allowed to get through. As soon as the bare minimum has been reached then any accusations of bias can be rebutted: "We can't be biased – look at the women we have appointed."

The discussions about the number of women on boards also frames what society sees as an acceptable outcome. Davies talks about 25%, and in Britain the 30% Club aims to achieve 30% female representation on boards. These numbers are the parameters of current discussion. If an organisation has a 15% female board then it is halfway to the 30% Club's target and nearly two-thirds of the way to reaching the Davies target. But who is to say these are the correct numbers? Why not 50%, or even 75%? If the "recommended target" was 50% then the organisation in our example would be feeling a little less satisfied with its progress.

The signs and symptoms listed in the gender bias field guide in Chapter 6 can be used to examine the way we do things at the policy, team and individual level. This approach and the actions described can be used for any process in an organisation. Practising this approach retrains our habitual ways of behaving and gives people the confidence to begin remaking the organisations in which they work.

Other actions

The example we have worked through shows that, by applying what we know about bias, we can look at situations afresh, question our assumptions and ensure we are looking at people as objectively as possible. There are also other actions we can take.

Empowerment and openness

Stereotypes, negative and positive, descriptive and prescriptive, are at the core of many decisions we make. Positive stereotypes and prescriptive stereotypes are particularly problematic with regard to gender. However, the solutions for dealing with different types of stereotype are likely to differ. As we have seen, descriptive gender stereotypes are best addressed by raising awareness of them. Prescriptive stereotypes need more sophisticated interventions. But having a bias isn't necessarily the problem: it is the willingness to do something about a bias that is. Once someone has become aware of the potential for bias in their decision-making and behaviour, how concerned are they about it? Some – perhaps many – will feel concerned enough to seek ways of tackling it. They will need awareness, understanding and a preparedness to change. This means more than sending someone on a training course, giving them a certificate and leaving them to it.

Research[2] suggests women may be able to counteract the effects of stereotype threat through fairly simply empowerment exercises. A series of experiments carried out by Fiske[2] used different techniques to make women feel powerful before taking maths tests. Since most people wrongly believe that women are poorer at maths than men, stereotype threat can act to make women underperform in line with expectations.

The empowerment techniques used were semantic priming, storytelling and positive memory exercises. In the first case, women were asked to form sentences from a set of words containing high-power and low-power terms. In the second experiment, they were asked to write about a time when they were either in power or under someone else's control. The third experiment involved doing memory tests of letter sequences. Those who felt high in power performed better on the maths tests than those who felt low in power and the control group. This was true even when the instructions for the maths test specifically highlighted the stereotype about women not being as good at maths as men.

This research shows that how we prepare ourselves prior to some kind of performance is not solely a matter of the technique or content being explicitly tested, but also depends on how well armed we are against biased thinking. The researchers point out that their methods do not make women any better at maths. The idea is to remove the influence of stereotype threat, to let natural ability flow. Thought exercises can act as a kind of performance enhancer by removing unconscious obstacles.

Gender bias needs to be incorporated into all forms of soft skill management and leadership training. Teamworking, recruitment, appraisal and communication training could all incorporate elements of gender bias training. We don't mean, of course, the "Let's appreciate each other's differences" approach to training – the "Women – what are they like!" approach. We mean making it explicit that gender bias has an impact on all forms of organisational life and that being aware of bias is the first step to tackling it.

Training needs to cover stereotyping. Discussing stereotypes reduces their activation. This seems antithetical to the usual approach to diversity today, where avoidance of such conversations is seen as not just the least risky approach but possibly even the correct moral choice. In this regard we, as practising psychologists, take an opposing stance to lawyers and some human resources (HR) practitioners. As a flavour of our approach, here is a case study we use in our work with clients.

Case Study : A colleague approaches you asking for help:

"We have just won a piece of work with a new client. The project will be very demanding and it will need attention 24/7. There are two people I have in mind to manage it. Monica, who has done this sort of work before, and Jane, who is less experienced but has potential. Monica has just returned from maternity leave, having had her first baby. I am thinking of going with Jane." Why do you think your colleague is thinking in this way, and what advice do you give your colleague?

The case study is designed to bring to light, and provoke discussion of, both descriptive and prescriptive stereotypes and to prompt participants to think about the actions they could take. The most common solution is that both Monica and Jane should be spoken to. While this is an understandable response, we question it. Prior to her maternity leave, Monica would have been given the new project automatically. Now, this would not necessarily have been the right decision. It might even have been unfair to Jane. But the idea of fairness would not even have been raised. Monica's motherhood is the trigger for considering fairness.

When we have presented this case to lawyers, they have said they would advise their colleague not to mention the baby when they meet with Monica. Presumably, the conversation would start with some bizarre question like, "So, Monica, tell me, what've you been up to the last 12 months?" This is almost surreal. And by being barred from discussing workplace arrangements, or readiness for taking on such work, the manager is almost forced into making assumptions. As long as these issues are not discussed openly and certainly not recorded, even in an email, then we have created the appearance of fairness while actually legislating against it.

This case study is about stereotypes and assumptions, and the difficulties we can experience when discussing such subjects. We need to loosen our reins a little so these sensitive topics can be aired. Lawyers don't want us to do so, and we respect their position. It's their job to protect the organisation. However, the research points us in the opposite direction – towards openness, honesty and self-examination. We accept that openly addressing gender bias runs the risk of enabling the reinforcement of gender stereotyping. It is not an exercise to be taken lightly or without preparation. However, avoiding the conversation won't make the problems go away. We must listen to each other and try to understand how our views on gender impact our decisions, actions and policies. If we don't, nothing will change.

Creating the right climate

The culture of the organisation is a key factor in whether or not gender diversity is taken seriously. There are several components to culture:

- Language: jargon, slang, gestures, signals, signs, humour, gossip, rumours, metaphors, proverbs and slogans

- Symbols: objects, natural and manufactured, settings, performers and functions

- Narratives: stories, legends, sagas, myths

- Practices: rituals, taboos, rites and ceremonies.[3]

All of these cultural components need to be examined. The myths about leadership are reflected in the leadership criteria, such as being courageous, innovative, pioneering, challenging and so on. Frankly, most people who have climbed the corporate ladder have done none of these things. They have got to where they are precisely because they *didn't* do any of these things. They are competent, bright and personable. It's time to let go of the hyperbolic myths about leaders. Malcolm Gladwell, in his *New Yorker* article "The Talent Myth", argued that people are given leadership positions not on performance but the *expectation* of performance.[4]

Leaders are clearly very important in setting the tone for an organisation. They need to be aware that they will be seen as role models on a topic such as gender equality. Overtly sexist language is taboo, but are leaders aware of the more subtle manifestations of gender bias? For example, take the pronoun "we". The ambiguity of "we" and "us" causes subtle reinforcement of prescriptive stereotypes. When "we" call for the inclusion of women, the identity of the speaker seems to be at least non-female, and therefore most likely male. This makes direct calls for inclusion seem self-confounding, however nobly they are put:

> If society is to be transformed to include real economic, legal and political equality, *we must include women* at decision-making tables.[5]
> If we want to bring the best of our clergy into the episcopate, *we must include women* in this order as well.[6]
> *We must include women* in peace processes and give them significant decision-making roles in conflict resolution.[7]

Matters would be clearer, if less elegant, if the speakers replaced "we must include women" with "men must stop excluding women and women must stop colluding with men's exclusion of women".

A further subtle problem with the "we must include" formulation is that it describes a future intention, rather than addressing a present problem. The situation we have inherited is sustained by habit. It's action that will change it, not statements. None of the institutions mentioned in the three above slogans is really challenged by these statements. They are easy to agree with – and ignore.

When messages about what it takes to get on in an organisation are presented in stereotypical descriptions we will get predictable results. When these messages are presented in a gender-neutral fashion (using terms such as "hard work", "motivation" or "aspiration") the results, in terms of an individual's self-perception, can be remarkable.

Social context influences both acceptance and recognition of behaviour. We are socialised to regard certain styles of interaction or presentation as appropriate for various settings. On the other hand, we associate these settings with a dominant gender. Sanctions act to reinforce stereotypes, encouraging people to behave according to prescribed gender norms and to reassert the idea that men and women are different. Our system of gender is circular, closed and self-supporting, as well as being unconsciously operated. No wonder it is so hard to grasp and examine, let alone challenge or change.

The future of work

Remarkably, much of today's work fits the mould originally cast for women's work. Computer-based work can be put down and picked up. Connectivity and mobile devices enable us to work in small time-slices integrated with our activities. As the distinction between work and home life begins to blur in an "always on" world, it may seem that we are losing something precious. Yet a more flexible attitude towards the allocation of our personal energies surely benefits us all.

Other trends in the workplace effectively challenge the maleness of the work culture we have inherited. Projects tend to be collaborative and to extend over time. Desperate fire-fighting is to be avoided in favour of predictability and a greater appreciation of the virtues of "business as usual". Teamwork is celebrated above individual heroics. People are expected to share knowledge rather than hoard it. Flatter management structures erode the militaristic flavour of hierarchical control. A greater focus in organisations on the needs of customers or citizens also favours the more supposedly "female" talents of empathy and imagination.

Contemporary work, then, is becoming feminised.[8] Rather than looking for a specific set of management skills, organisations are looking for a particular kind of person. The worker is expected to be the embodiment of the organisation. She may be asked to "live the values" of the organisation and will almost certainly be expected to profess "passion" for whatever the organisation makes or does. In both public and private sector organisations, understanding the needs and drives of the customer has become paramount. The supposedly feminine capacity for empathy is therefore at a premium. Today's employee must think like a consumer, and ideally be an actual consumer of the organisation.

This is especially true in retail, one of the most feminised – and psychologised – areas of contemporary business. Why and how people buy are seen as questions more suited to female thinking habits. Additionally, it's as consumers that we find our identity. Shopping for fashions, furnishings and food is a means of boosting self-esteem and a focus for building self-identity.

Since consumption has become the motor of the economy, so the feminisation of consumption strikes at the heart of our culture:

> Because both shopping and looking good have traditionally been feminised concerns, it is not simply that the new worker is feminised but that the relationship between work and play, production and consumption, has been feminised.[8]

At the same time, structural changes in the economy tend to highlight what are seen as feminine traits. The decline of mass manufacturing shifts emphasis towards personalisation of products on the one hand, and greater investment in service industries on the other. Globalisation tends to detach traditional roles from localities, undermining gendered patterns: when a steel town ceases to make steel, it ceases to be male. (In the film *The Full Monty*, unemployed Sheffield steel workers turn to stripping as a way of making money instead.) Automated technology and connectivity, together with an accelerated business cycle and investment uncertainty, have led to the casualisation of work. The "job for life" has gone, placing the concept of "the job" in question for the first time since the triumph of the Industrial Revolution.

But to say that work is becoming more female could be to repeat the mistakes of the past. What seems to be happening is that the reality of contemporary work has the potential to be detached from a male-built design. The emerging work culture might be better described as neutral or ungendered, rather than female. We need to escape from the oppositions of gender, rather than seeking redress for past wrongs – which is, in any case, a stereotypically male response to a perceived attack on status.

Reactions to feminisation

Not everyone is happy with the idea that work is becoming feminised. Some of the least happy are women, which shows that the gradual, multi-generational indoctrination which has shaped our mental models is no discriminator.

Yahoo's chief executive Marissa Mayer caused a stir in 2013 when she insisted that employees no longer work from home on a permanent basis.[9] Mayer came from Google, so her digital economy credentials aren't in question. She is also a mother, so she should know a thing or two about work–life balance. One of the reasons stated for the new ruling was that Yahoo needs the unstructured, impromptu encounters that happen in offices. This sounds odd, given that web-based companies are predicated on the extension of collaborative relationships across networks. Critics suggested Mayer wanted to reduce headcount, and therefore passively fired anyone who wanted to continue to work from home. Other people claimed that home-workers were less productive – a suspicion that has dogged the idea of home-working ever since technology made it possible to reintroduce this pre-industrial option. Communications company Vodafone pitched in with the claim that home-working saves organisations money, the average corporate desk costing £5,746 per year.[10]

These rational arguments seem to miss the central point about the home-working dispute, which is that challenging the traditional divide between home and workplace causes many people a great deal of discomfort. It may not be up there with same-sex marriage, but some people clearly think that the home/work divide is divinely ordained, or that the purity of the home – or the sanctity of the workplace – is threatened by such transgressive behaviour. No one would put it like that, but such sentiments lurk beneath the rationalised arguments.

Language, too, is struggling with feminisation. "The breadwinner" is singular and male. A family is not supposed to have more than one breadwinner, and the breadwinner can't be a woman. The following piece of news comes not from 1912, but 2012: "The advent of female breadwinning is seen by some as a crime against nature."[11] The same article claims that "the word 'purse-whipped' — referring to men being in financial thrall to women — is slowly entering the English language", though there doesn't seem to be a citation for the word any earlier than a flurry of newspaper pieces in September 2012. The language being used here suggests a general societal move, a groundswell of opinion, but the only evidence is anecdotal. Do we really see female breadwinners as unnatural, or is this just what some newspapers want us to think?

The aspect of work that would seem closest to the phenomenon of feminisation is the growth of part-time working. Part-time working is seen as a way of adapting traditions of work to women's lives. In fact, part-time working is part of the problem, not the solution. This is because the system surrounding the part-time worker has not changed to accommodate it. So, a female executive working three days a week is still expected to be as productive as her full-time colleague, yet is also suspected of less-than-complete dedication to the organisation. Business processes don't flex around part-time workers' schedules. Such workers do not get compensatory support for the missed continuity that their fragmented work week brings them. For part-time work to make a meaningful difference in our lives and our businesses, it needs to be taken into account in the overall design of the organisation, not treated as an optional afterthought that disrupts the smooth running of the organisation. Perhaps "part-timer" will then no longer be regularly used as a jokingly derogatory term for someone who arrives late.

As part-time workers are usually women, women become less noticeable in the workplace. Their absence is then justified or rationalised in various (negative) ways: they are less committed, or less able. Part-time working therefore reinforces the notion of women as exceptions at work – even though it is designed to promote inclusion.

Genuine work flexibility demands that we rethink work as a whole. We need to dismantle the machine we inherited and ask what structures, processes and relationships we need to put in place for the modern world. We also need to question the centrality of the engineering paradigm. There are other models that may suit organisational design better – models drawn from disciplines such as biology, town planning and network theory, perhaps; and models based on what we know about human behaviours and values.

Government and legislation can help here. Certainly the introduction of parental leave, following the lead of Scandinavian countries, will make a difference. Allowing parents to share caring for their newborn will assist in changing attitudes to childcare. Governments can also insist that public companies report on any gender pay gaps in their organisations. Focusing their efforts in these areas will help to change mindsets – or help to continue that process.

Writers and thinkers who have examined the future of work have concluded that, although the world of work is changing, our attitudes towards gender are adapting far more slowly. In their book *Future Work*,[12] Alison Maitland and Peter Thomson acknowledge the importance of legislation on flexible working but also feel there is a more fundamental problem to be addressed: "We need an urgent reframing of careers and career development, because women's career paths tend to be very different from the traditional male model that still prevails in many organisations."

It is our attitudes that constitute the biggest obstacle. In his book *The Future of Work*,[13] Richard Donkin makes a similar observation: "It is a supreme irony for women that at the very time their career prospects appear healthier than they have been at any stage in history, with better education, greater opportunities and various anti-discriminatory safeguards, they are being urged to reflect on their family responsibilities."

As work becomes more collaborative and the importance of diversity becomes more obvious, we are perhaps looking at a return to an earlier way of life rather than a breakthrough to something new. History may judge our rigidly gendered world as an interlude or as a regressive period on the journey towards a more productive and fulfilling society. While we must not romanticise pre-industrial times, there was nevertheless a pattern of women and men working side by side, sharing work according to context rather than a textbook. This looks much more like the emerging collaborative workplace than any rejigged "men first" hierarchical approach.

Making a new world of work

History doesn't repeat itself, said Mark Twain, but it does rhyme. Our ignorance of the history of work means we live under the comforting assumption that, as far as gender equality at work is concerned, we have far more egalitarian attitudes than any previous generation. As we have seen in this book, there was a time when women were able to engage in a wider range of occupations than they do now and when society was more equal. The organisations of today rhyme with those created in the past. These rhymes are powerful and insistent and, unless we acknowledge and oppose the power of gender bias, they will continue into the future.

Can we unpick the patterns that we have learned and reproduced? Are we ready to step out from behind our comforting, but erroneous, ideas about gender? Do we really want our organisations to be better places – for all their staff? It's up to each and every one of us.

References

1. Heilman ME, Haynes MC. 'No credit where credit is due: Attributional rationalization of women's success in male–female teams.' *Journal of Applied Psychology* 2005; 90(5): 905–916. doi:10.1037/0021-9010.90.5.905.

2. Fiske STS. 'Controlling other people. The impact of power on stereotyping.' *American Psychologist* 1993; 48(6): 621–628.

3. Trice HM, Beyer JM. *The Cultures of Work Organizations*. Pearson; 1993.

4. Available at: http://www.newyorker.com/archive/2002/07/22/020722fa_fact. Accessed 23 September 2013.

5. Leadership Summit for Women 2012. Available at: www.facebook.comevents/428690287191868/. Accessed 23 September 2013.

6. The Bishop of Salisbury, the Right Reverend Nicholas Holtam, speaking at the Church of England Synod in November 2012. Available at: http://www.christiantoday.co.uk/article/church.of.england.defeat.for.women.bishops.legislation/31094.htm. Accessed 23 September 2013.

7. Ambassador Brooke D. Anderson, US Alternate Representative for Special Political Affairs, speaking at the UN in July 2010. Available at: http://usun.state.gov/briefing/statements/2010/144792.htm. Accessed 23 September 2013.

8. Walkerdine V, Jimenez L. *Gender, Work and Community After De-Industrialisation*. Palgrave Macmillan; 2012. doi:10.1057/9780230359192.

9. Available at: http://www.telegraph.co.uk/finance/newsbysector/mediatechnologyandtelecoms/9892282/Yahoo-boss-bans-working-from-home.html. Accessed 23 September 2013.

10. Available at: http://www.telegraph.co.uk/finance/jobs/9920874/Vodafone-fights-back-against-Yahoo-working-from-ban.html. Accessed 23 September 2013.

11. Available at: http://www.dailymail.co.uk/femail/article-2200020/Women-bread-winners--transform-aspect-lives.html. Accessed 23 September 2013.

12. Maitland A, Thomson P. *Future Work*. Palgrave Macmillan; 2011.

13. Donkin R. *The Future of Work*. Palgrave Macmillan; 2009.

Index

Entries in *italics* denote illustrations or tables

Credits

Chapter 1

Fig 1.1: Women building city walls from Christine de Pizan, Le Livre de la Cite des Dames (early 15th century). Bibliothèque Nationale de France.

Fig 1.2: A woman working on an aircraft propeller World War 1 ©Imperial War Musueum

Chapter 2

Fig 2.1:Woman sculptor from Boccaccio, Le Livre des Cleres et Nobles Femmes (early 15th century). Bibliothèque Nationale de France.

Fig 2.2: Women's football, 26 December 1920, Goodison Park, Liverpool. Source unknown.

Chapter 3

Table 3.1: Commonly held gender stereotypes. adapted from Rudman, Greenwald and McGhee, 2001.

Fig 3.1: The Impact of Context © Mike Idziaszczyk

Chapter 4

Fig 4.1: Hilary Clinton. Associated Press, Elise Amendola. ©PA Images

Fig 4.2: Julia Gillard. Getty Images, Scott Barbour © Getty Images News

Chapter 5

Table 5.1: Gender and Leadership from Burke, E. & Glennon, R. The SHL Talent Report. © SHL US